Perth and Perthshire REGISTER for 1921

containing
Lists of the Nobility, the Institutions
of the City and County, and County
Council Administration

Glasgow
The Grimsay Press
2003

The Grimsay Press
an imprint of
Zeticula
57 St Vincent Crescent
Glasgow
G3 8NQ

http://www.thegrimsaypress.co.uk
admin@thegrimsaypress.co.uk

Transferred to digital printing in 2003

Copyright © Zeticula 2003

First published in Great Britain 1920

ISBN 0 902664 60 3

Perth and Perthshire Register.

NOBILITY.

DUKES (2).

(QUEEN ANNE, 1703)—JOHN-GEORGE STEWART MURRAY, DUKE OF ATHOLL, Baron Murray of Tullibardine, 1604, Earl of Tullibardine, Baron Gask, Baron Balquhidder, 1606, Earl of Atholl, 1629, Marquis of Atholl, Viscount Balquhidder, Baron Balvenie, 1676, Duke of Atholl, Marquis of Tullibardine, Earl of Strathtay, Earl of Strathardle, Viscount Glenalmond, Viscount Glenlyon, 1703, Peerage of Scotland; Baron Strange of Knockyn, 1628, Peerage of England; Baron Percy, 1722, Earl Strange, Baron Murray of Stanley, 1786, Peerage of G. B.; Baron Glenlyon, 1821, Peerage of United Kingdom; born 15th December, 1871; M.V.O., D.S.O. (1898), C.B. (1917); Brig.-General Commanding Scottish Horse, Hon. Colonel 10th Scottish Battn. The King's (Liverpool Regiment); D.L., Lord Lieutenant, and President of the Territorial Association of Perthshire; was M.P. for West Perthshire 1910-17; Lord High Commissioner and K.T., 1918; married 1899, Katherine Marjory, daughter of Sir James Ramsay, Bart., of Bamff; succ. his father, the 7th Duke, 1917. His Lordship's surviving sisters and brothers are:—Lady Dorothea-Louisa, born 25th March, 1866, married February, 1895, Major-General H. G. Ruggles-Brise; Lady Helen, born 20th April, 1867, married December, 1916, D. A Tod, Esq., of Braehead; Lady Evelyn, born 17th March, 1868. Lord James Thomas, Captain, The Cameron Highlanders, born 18th August, 1879. The ancient Baronies of Strange, &c., 1299, fell in abeyance in 1594, on the death of Ferdinand, 5th Earl of Derby. Seats—Blair Castle and Dunkeld House, Perthshire. Residence in London—84 Eaton Place, S.W, 1.

(QUEEN ANNE, 1707)—DOUGLAS-BERESFORD-MALISE-RONALD GRAHAM, DUKE OF MONTROSE, K.T., Marquis of Graham and Buchanan, Earl of Kincardine; Earl and Baron Graham of G. B. 1722; 1916-17, Lord High Commissioner to the General Assembly of the Church of Scotland; late Lieutenant 5th Lancers; late Colonel 3rd Battalion Argyle and Sutherland Highlanders; A.D.C. to the King; Lord Lieutenant of Stirlingshire; son of James, 4th Duke; born 1852; succeeded his father as 5th Duke, 1874; married 1876, Miss Violet Hermione, 2nd daughter of Sir Frederick and Lady Graham of Netherby, and has issue—James, Marquis of Graham, born 1878; married 1906, Lady Mary Hamilton, and has issue. James Angus Earl of Kincardine, born 1907, Lady Mary Helen Alma, born 1909, Lord Ronald Malise Hamilton, born 1912; Lady Helen Violet, born 1879; Lady Hermione Emily, born 1882; married 1906, D. Cameron of Lochiel, and has issue; Lord Douglas Malise. D.S.O, M.C., Major, R.A., born 1883; Lord Alastair Mungo. Lieut.-Commander R.N., born 1886; m. 1916, Lady Muriel, only daughter of 7th Earl Bathurst, and has issue. Seat—Buchanan Castle, Stirlingshire.

MARQUIS (1).
MARQUIS OF BREADALBANE.

GAVIN CAMPBELL, OF BREADALBANE, K.G., 1677 Marquis of Breadalbane and Holland, Viscount of Tay and Paintland, Baron Glenorchy, Benederaloch, Ormelie and Weik; in the Peerage of the United Kingdom, 1873 Baron Breadalbane of Kenmore, 1885 Marquis of Breadalbane and Earl of Ormelie; 1625 a baronet of Scotland and Nova Scotia; 1873-4 Lord in Waiting to Queen Victoria; 1875 a Deputy-Lieutenant and 1914 Lord-Lieutenant of Argyllshire, of which County his lordship is also a County Councillor and President of the Territorial Association, as well as a J.P. and County Councillor of Perthshire; 1880 a Privy Councillor; 1880-5 Treasurer, and 1892-5 Lord Steward of the Queen's Household; 1893-5 H.M.'s Lord High Commissioner to the General Assembly of the Church of Scotland; 1893 K.G.; 1903 aide-de-camp to the King; was a Lieutenant in the 4th Bn. Argyll and Sutherland Highlanders, and Captain Shropshire Yeomanry Cavalry; is Lt.-Gen. in the King's Body-Guard for Scotland, and a member of the Fishery Board; was Col. Highland Cyclist Bn. Territorial Force (now Hon. Col.); was a Military Member of the Territorial Force Association for Perthshire; born 1851; succeeded his father, 1871; married 1872, Lady Alma Imogen Leonora-Carlotta, daughter of James 4th Duke of Montrose. Seats— Taymouth Castle, Aberfeldy, Perthshire; Craig, Dalmally, Argyllshire. London Residence—68 Ennismore Gardens, S.W.7 Clubs,—Reform, Brooks, and National Liberal.

EARLS (12).

WALTER-JOHN-FRANCIS ERSKINE, EARL OF MAR and KELLIE. 1429, Baron Erskine; 1565, Earl of Mar; 1603, Baron Dirleton; 1606, Viscount Fentoun; 1619, Earl of Kellie; Premier Viscount of Scotland; 1892 a Representative Peer; is Lord-Lieutenant; Convener, and President of the Territorial Association of Clackmannanshire; 1909 a Brigadier in the King's Body Guard for Scotland; 1911 K.T.; born 1865; succeeded his father 1888; Hon. Colonel 7th Battalion (Princess (Louise's) Argyll and Sutherland Highlanders. Married 1892 Lady Susan Violet Ashley, daughter of Anthony 8th Earl of Shaftesbury, and has had issue, Lady Elyne-Violet, born and died 1893; John F. A., Lord Erskine, born 1895, Lieutenant Scots Guards; Hon. Francis Walter, born 1899; 2nd Lieut. Scots Guards. Seat—Alloa House, Clackmannanshire.

MAR, EARL OF, JOHN-FRANCIS-ERSKINE GOODEVER-ERSKINE, 1404, Earl of Mar and Baron Garioch; 1886, Representative Peer; born 1836; succeeded in 1866 his uncle. John-Francis-Miller Erskine, Earl of Mar and Earl of Kellie, in the titles Earl of Mar and Baron Garioch. The finding of the Committee of Privileges in 1875 regarding the Earldom of Mar of 1565, claimed by the Earl of Kellie, having given rise to doubts whether the ancient dignity had not been by some means "surrendered or merged in the Crown," an Act of Parliament was passed in 1885 to remove these doubts by confirming the old title as fully as if there had been no such surrender. Married, 1866, Alice-Mary Sinclair, elder daughter of the late John Hamilton, Esq., of Hilston Park, Monmouthshire, and has issue John-Francis-Hamilton-Sinclair-Cunliffe-Brooks-Forbes, Lord Garioch, born 1868, married 1903 Sybil, daughter of R. Heath-cote, of Manton, Rutlandshire. Residence—Villa Indiana, Monte Carlo. London Residence—17 Dover Street, W.1. Clubs—Carlton, and Scottish London, S.W.

(QUEEN MARY, 1562)—MORTON - GRAY STUART, EARL OF MORAY; 1562, Earl of Moray; 1581, Baron Doune; 1611, Baron St. Colme; in the Peerage of Great Britain, 1796, Baron Stuart of Castle Stuart; M.A. (Camb.); a J.P. for Perthshire; born 1855; succeeded his brother, Francis James, 16th Earl, 1909; married 1890, Edith-Douglas, daughter of Rear-Admiral George Palmer, and has issue–Hon. Francis-Douglas, Lord Doune, M.C., born 1892, Flight Commander, R.F.C.; Hon. Archibald John Morton, born 1894; Hon. James Gray, M.C., born 1897, Captain Royal Scots; Lady Hermione Moray, born 1899, m. 1919 Capt. H. T. Buller, C.B., M.V.O., R.N. Seats—Donibristle Park, Fifeshire; Darnaway Castle, Moray-shire; Castle Stuart, Inverness-shire; Doune Lodge, Perth-shire. Residences—Kinfauns Castle, Perthshire; and Gray House, Forfarshire.

(JAMES VI., 1601)—EDWARD - JAMES BRUCE, EARL OF ELGIN AND KINCARDINE, Baron Bruce of Kinloss, 1603; Earl of Elgin and Baron Bruce of Kinloss, 1633; Earl of Kincardine and Baron Bruce of Torry, in the Peerage of Scot-land, 1647; Baron Elgin of Elgin, 1849, in the Peerage of the United Kingdom; J.P., D.L., and Member of Territorial Force Association of Fife; Major Highland (Fifeshire) R.G.A., Assistant Director of Labour, B.E.F., France, with temporary rank of Lieut.-Col., 1917; born 1881, succeeded his father 1917. His Lordship's surviving sisters and brothers are—Lady Elizabeth Mary, born 1877 (married 1898, Sir H. Babington Smith, K.C.B., C.S.I.); Lady Christian Augusta b. 1879 (m. 1904, Sir Herbert Ogilvy of Inver-quharity, 12th Bart.); Lady Constance Veronica, b. 1880; Hon. Robert, b. 1882; Major 11th Hussars; m. 1910. Katherine, only child of General the Hon. John E. Lindley and has issue; Hon. David, Captain Seaforth Highlanders, b. 1888; Lady Rachel Catherine, b. 1890; m. 1911 Sir Harry Verney, Bart., M.P., of Claydon, Buckingham-shire; Hon. John Bernard, Lieut. R.N., b. 1892; Hon. Victor, b. 1897, Lieut. 11th Hussars; and Hon. Bernard, b. 1917 (posthumous issue by second marriage. Seat—Broomhall, Fifeshire.

(JAMES VI., 1605)—WILLIAM-HUNTLY DRUMMOND, 15th EARL OF PERTH, and 8th Viscount of Strathallan, Hereditary Thane of Lennox, 1070; Lord Stobhall, 1315; Hereditary Steward of Menteith, 1250, and Strathern, 1473; Lord Drum-mond, 1487; Earl of Perth and Lord Drummond of Stobhall and Montifex, 1605. Born 1871; succeeded as Viscount of Strathallan in 1893 on death of his father, 7th Viscount; and as Earl of Perth, etc., on death of 14th Earl in 1902. The 7th Viscount of Strathallan married (1) Ellen, daughter of C. B. Thornhill, Esq., C.S.I., by whom there was issue the 8th Vis-count; and (2) Margaret, daughter of William Smythe of

Methven, by whom there were issue—Sir James Eric, K.C.M.G.,
b. 1876, m. 1904, Hon Angela-Mary younger daughter of the
11th Lord Herries, and has issue; Maurice Charles Andrew,
D S.O., Major, the Black Watch; b. 1877, m 1904, Miss Ida
Drummond, and has issue; Margaret Cicely, b. 1880; m. 1912,
Alfred B. S. Tennyson; Sybil Frances, b. 1881; Edmund
Rupert, b. 1884, Commander R.N., m. 1910, Evelyn Frances,
elder daughter of Lord Arthur Butler, and has issue.

(CHARLES 1., 1633)— GEORGE-HARLEY HAY, EARL OF
KINNOULL Viscount Dupplin, etc., Baron Hay of Ped-.
wardine, G.B., 1711; born 1902; succeeded his grandfather,
Archibald, 12th Earl, 1916, who was born 1855; succeeded
1897; died 1916, having married (1st) 1879, Josephine
Maria (died 1900), second daughter of the late John Hawke,
Esq. (judicial separation in 1885.) (2nd), 1903, Florence Mary,
youngest daughter of late Edward Darrell, Esq. Issue (by 1st
marriage) EDMUND ALFRED ROLLO GEORGE, VISCOUNT DUPPLIN,
born 1879, died 1903, leaving a son, the present Earl.
(By 2nd marriage), Lady Elizabeth Blanche Mary,
born 1903, and Lady Margaret Florence Grace, born 1907,
Seat—Balhousie Castle, Perthshire.

(CHARLES I., 1633)—HUGO-RICHARD WEMYSS-CHARTERIS-
DOUGLAS, EARL OF WEMYSS AND MARCH. 1628 Baron
Wemyss of Elcho, 1633 Earl of Wemyss, Baron Elcho and
Methil, 1697 Earl of March, Viscount of Peebles, and Baron
Douglas of Neidpath, Lyne, and Munard; in the Peerage of
the U.K., 1821 Baron Wemyss of Wemyss; 1625 a Baronet of
Scotland and Nova Scotia; 1883-85 M.P. for Haddingtonshire;
1886-95 M.P. for Ipswich; is a Deputy-Lieutenant of Peebles
(1890) and Lord Lieutenant of Haddington (1918); b. 1857;
succeeded his father, Francis, 9th Earl of Wemyss and 6th Earl
of March, 1914; m. 1883 Mary-Constance, eldest daughter of the
late Hon. Percy-Scawen Wyndham, and has issue—(1) Hugo-
Francis, Lord Elcho. b. 1884; killed in action 1916, having m.
1911 Lady Violet Manners, second daughter of the 8th Duke of
Rutland, and left issue—1. FRANCIS DAVID ELCHO, b. 1912;
2. Hon. MARTIN MICHAEL CHARLES, b. 1913. (2) Hon. Guy, b.
1886, m. 1912 Frances Lucy, eldest daughter of Francis J.
Tennant, and has issue. (3) Lady Cynthia, b. 1887, m. 1910
Herbert, son of the Right Hon. H. H. Asquith, ex-Prime Minister,
and has issue. (4) Hon. Colin, b. 1889, d. 1892. (5) Lady Mary,
b. 1895. (6) Hon. Ivo Alan, b. 1896, 2nd Lieut Grenadier Guards,
killed in action Oct. 17, 1915. (7) Lady Irene-Corona, b. 1902.
Seats—Gosford House, Seton and Amisfield, Haddington;
Elcho Castle, Perthshire; Stanway, Gloucestershire; Neidpath Castle, Barns, Peeblesshire; London Residence—23
St. James Place, S.W.1.

(CHARLES I., 1639)—DAVID-LYULPH-GORE-WOLSELEY OGILVY,
EARL OF AIRLIE, M.C., Captain 10th Hussars, born 1893,
succeeded his father 1900; married 1917, Lady Alexandra-
Maria-Bridget Coke, younger daughter of the 6th Earl of
Leicester, and has issue — two daughters Seats — Airlie
and Cortachy Castles; Tulchan of Glenisla; Auchterhouse
and Downie Park. Forfarshire.

(James VII., 1686)– Alexander-Edward Murray, EARL of
DUNMORE, Viscount Fincastle; Baron Murray of Blair-
Moulin and Tullimet; in the Peerage of the United Kingdom
1831 Baron Dunmore of Dunmore, in the Forest of Atholl;
1895-97 A.D.C. to Viceroy of India (Earl of Elgin); served with
Soudan Field Force in 1896, with Malakand Field Force, 1897-8
(medal with clasp and V.C.), and in South Africa, 1899-1900, with
16th Lancers (mentioned in despatches); commanded the 31st
Bn. Imperial Yeomanry in 1902 (with temporary rank of Lieut.-
Colonel); 1906 M.V.O.; is Major 16th Lancers; G.S.O., 3rd
grade, in France; 1914 a Deputy Lieutenant for the County
of Inverness; b. 1871; suc. his father 1907; m. 1904
Lucinda Dorothea, eldest daughter of Horace Kemble,
Esq., of Knock, Isle of Skye, and has issue—1. Lady
Marjory Hilda, b. 1904.; 2. Edward David, Viscount
Fincastle. b. 1908; 3. Lady Mary Elizabeth, b. 1913. His lord-
ship's father, Charles-Adolphus, 7th earl, b. 1841, m. 1866 Lady
Gertrude, third daughter of Thomas William, 2nd Earl
of Leicester, and left issue—1. Lady Evelyn, b. 1867, m.
1891 John D. Cobbold, Esq., of Holy Wells, Suffolk,
and has issue. 2. Lady Muriel, b. 1869, m. 1890 Colonel
H. Gore-Browne, The King's Royal Rifle Corps, son of
Sir Thomas Gore-Browne, c.b. 3. The present earl. 4. Lady
Grace, b. 1873, m. 1896 William James Tress Barry, Esq.,
son of the late Sir Francis Tress Barry, Bt., and has issue. 5.
Lady Victoria-Alexandrina. b. 1877. 6. Lady Mildred, b. 1878, m.
1904 Gilbert B. S. Follett, D.S.O., Major Coldstream Guards.
Seat, Isle of Harris, Inverness-shire   London Residence. 33
Gloucester Square, W.2

MANSFIELD, Earl of, Alan-David Murray, late Captain
Black Watch; 1605, Baron Scone; 1621, Viscount Stormont;
1641, Baron Balvaird; in the Peerage of Great Britain, 1776,
Earl of Mansfield in the County of Notts, and 1792, Earl of
Mansfield, in the County of Middlesex; D.L. for County
of Perth, and County Commandant of Perthshire
Volunteers; J.P. for Counties of Perth, Dumfries and
Clackmannan; County Council Representative in the
Territorial Force Association of Perthshire, born 1864;
succeeded his brother, William-David, 10th Viscount and
5th Earl of Mansfield, in the County of Middlesex, and 4th Earl
of Mansfield in the County of Notts, 1906. His Lordship married
April, 1899. Margaret-Helen-Mary, daughter of the late Rear-
Admiral Sir Malcolm MacGregor of MacGregor, Bart., and
has issue—Mungo-David-Malcolm, Lord Scone, born 9th
August, 1900. His Lordship's father, William-David, Viscount
Stormont, D.L. co., Dumfries, and Vice-Lieutenant co. Perth,
A.D.C. to the Queen, Colonel Commanding 3rd Batt. Black
Watch, formerly Lieutenant Grenadier Guards, born 1835
(married 1857, Emily Louisa, eldest daughter of Sir John
Atholl MacGregor, 3rd Bart. of MacGregor), died 1893, leaving
issue—William-David, late Earl of Mansfield; Lady Marjory-
Louisa, born 1862 (married 1891, Sir Kenneth J. Mackenzie of
Gairloch, Bart.); Hon. Andrew-David, Capt. and Brevet-Lieut.-

Colonel Queen's Own Cameron Highlanders, commanded Lovat's Scouts, born 1863, killed South Africa, 1901; Hon. Alan-David, the present Peer; Lady Mabel-Emily, born 1866 (married 1905, Rear-Admiral Herbert G. King-Hall, R.N., D.S.O.); Hon. Angus-David, Lieut. R.N., born 1869, died 1898; Hon. Alexander-David, Captain 3rd Battalion Black Watch, born 1871, married 1908, Christian Maule Stewart Richardson, daughter of the late Sir James Stewart Richardson, Bart. of Pitfour. Seats—Scone Palace and Logiealmond, Perthshire; Comlongon Castle, Dumfriesshire, and Schaw Park, Clackmannanshire.

CAMPERDOWN, EARL of, GEORGE ALEXANDER PHILIPS HALDANE HALDANE-DUNCAN; 1797, Viscount Duncan of Camperdown and Baron Duncan of Lundie in the Peerage of Great Britain; 1831, Earl of Camperdown of Camperdown, and of Gleneagles, in that of the United Kingdom; b. 1845; succeeded his brother, Robert, 3rd Earl and 4th Viscount, 1867; married 1888 Laura (d. 1910), daughter of John Dove, Esq. His Lordship's father, born 1812, married 1839 Juliana Cavendish, born 1821, eldest daughter of Sir George R. Philips, Bart., and had issue—(1) Lady Julia-Janet-Georgiana, born 1840, married 1858 George Ralph, 4th Baron Abercromby; (2) the late Peer; (3) the present Peer.

VISCOUNTS (2).

STRATHALLAN, VISCOUNT. See PERTH, Earl of.

HALDANE, VISCOUNT—RICHARD BURDON HALDANE; 1911, Viscount Haldane of Cloan; 1913, K.T., M.A., K.C., LL.D., son of the late Robert Haldane, Esq., W.S., of Cloan, Perthshire, by Mary Elizabeth, daughter of the late Richard Burdon Sanderson, Esq., of Otterburn, Northumberland; born 1856; educated at Edinburgh University and at Gottingen; called to the English Bar, 1879; K.C., 1890; P.C., 1902; 1915 Order of Merit; Lord Rector of Edinburgh University, 1905-1908; Secretary of State for War 1905-1912; LL.D., Cambridge University, 1907; Lord High Chancellor, 1912-15; was M.P. for the County of Haddington, 1885-1911. Residences—Cloan, near Auchterarder, Scotland. 28 Queen Anne's Gate, London, S.W.1 Clubs—New and Liberal, Edinburgh; Brook's, Athenæum, and National Liberal, London.

BARONS (9).

(CHARLES I., 1643)—MONTOLIEU-FOX OLIPHANT-MURRAY, LORD ELIBANK in the Peerage of Scotland, Baronet of Scotland an 1 N. S. 1628; Viscount Elibank in the Peerage of the United Kingdom, 1911; Com. Royal Navy, retired, son of Alexander, 9th Lord, by Emily Maria, only daughter of Archibald Montgomery, Esq. of Whim, born 27th April, 1840; succeeded his father 1871, married 1868 Blanche Alice, eldest daughter of the late E lward John Scott, Esq. of Portland Lodge, Southsea, Hants. Issue, Helen Emily, born 1869, died

1870; Right Hon. Alexander William Charles Oliphant, Master of Elibank (now Baron Murray of Elibank), 1909 Under-Secretary for India; 1910-12 Patronage Secy. to the Treasury; was M.P. for Mid-Lothian 1900-5 and 1910-12, and for Peebles and Selkirk 1906-10; born 12th April, 1870 (*m.* 1894, Miss Hilda Wolfe Murray); (*d.* 13th Sept., 1920); Hon. Edward Oliphant, born 22nd Oct., 1871, Captain Cameron Highlanders, Adjutant Lovat's Scouts, killed South Africa, 1901; married 1900, Minnie, daughter of Allhusen, Esq; Emily Blanche, born 20th Dec., 1872 (*m.* 1893, Sir R. Grenville Harvey, Bart.); Alice Florence, born 2nd Dec. 1873; Nina Charlotte, born 7th April, 1875 (*m.* 1896, H. Philipson); CHARLES GIDEON, born 7th Aug., 1877, M.P. for St. Rollox Division of Glasgow since 1918 (*m.* 1908, Ermine Mary, daughter of the Hon. Mrs Madocks, and widow of Lieut.-Col. Aspinwall); Arthur Cecil, D.S.O., born 27th March, 1879, M.P. for Kincardineshire since 1908; Clara Isabel, born October 24th, 1880 (*m.* 1902, Hon. Oswald Partington); James Oliphant, born 21st Aug., 1882, died 1885; Hon. Evelyn-Izme, born 1886, married (1) 1906, George (died 1916), only son of Sir Charles N. Nicholson, M.P., London. (2) 1917, Rht. Hon. J. E. Seely, D.S.O., M.P. Seats—Darn Hall, Peeblesshire; Ballencrieff, East Lothian; Pitheavlis, Perthshire; Elibank, Selkirkshire.

(CHARLES II., 1651)—WILLIAM-CHARLES-WORDSWORTH ROLLO, LORD ROLLO in the Peerage of Scotland, and BARON DUNNING in the Peerage of the United Kingdom; Lieut.-Colonel 3rd Royal Highlanders; a Brigadier of the King's Body Guard for Scotland; born 8th Jan., 1860; succeeded his father, JOHN-ROGERSON, 10th baron, 1916; (married 21st March, 1882, Mary Eleanor, 3rd daughter of Captain Beaumont W. Hotham); and has issue—Hon. Rosalind-Mary-Agnes, born 1896. His lordship's father was born 1835, succeeded his father 1852; married 1857, Agnes Bruce (died 1906), daughter of Lieut.-Col. Trotter of Ballindean, and had issue— Hon. Agnes-Catherine, *b.* 1858, *m.* 1883, the Rev. R. M. G. Browne. The present peer; Hon. Eric Norman, born 1861 (married 1888, Constance Hohler); Hon. Constance Agnes, born 1862; Hon. Herbert Evelyn, born 1864, died 1893; Hon. (Bernard Francis, born 1868; Hon. Cecily Agatha Agnes, born 1870; Hon. Gilbert de St. Croix, born 13th Aug. 1872 married, 1904, Margaret Antrobus); Hon. Elizabeth-Theresa-Agnes, *b.* 1874, *d.* 1875. Seats –Duncrub Park, Perthshire; Duncrieff House, Dumfriesshire.

(CHARLES II., 1682) –WALTER-JAMES-HORE-RUTHVEN BARON RUTHVEN,; 1651, Baron Ruthven of Freeland, created Baron Ruthven of Gowrie in the Peerage of the United Kingdom 1919, late Rifle Brigade; Grand Officier de la Couronne Belge; King's Messenger for the duration of the War; is a Deputy-Lieutenant of Perthshire and a J.P. for Lanarkshire and Herefordshire; born 1838; succeeded his grandmother, Baroness Ruthven; 1864; married 1869, Lady Caroline Gore (died 1915), daughter of the Earl of Arran; issue the MASTER OF RUTHVEN, C.M.G.; D.S.O., born 1870, Brig.-Gen. 1st Guards Brigade; Hon. Alexander Gore, born 1872, V.C., D.S.O., Brig.-Gen. 2nd Guards Brigade, G.S.O.

1/62nd Division; Hon. Christian Malise. C.M.G., D.S.O.
born 1880, Major Black Watch; G.S.O., 2nd Canadian
Division in France; Hon. Philip James Leslie, born 1882,
died 1908; having married 1906 Lydia-Gladys, daughter
of Henry Adams of Cannon Hill, Maidenhead. His Lordship's father, eldest son of the late Baroness and Walter
Hore Ruthven of Harperstown, county Wexford (married 1836,
Della Honoria, daughter of Colonel Lowen, K. H.) died 1847,
leaving, besides the present Lord, a son and two daughters.
Seats—Newland, Midlothian. Harperstown county Wexford.
Residence—11 Clarges Street. Piccadilly, London, W.1.

(CHARLES II., 1682)—ARTHUR FITZGERALD, LORD KIN-
NAIRD; Baron Kinnaird of Rossie, U.K.,1860; son of Arthur,
10th Lord by Mary Jane, daughter of William Henry Hoare,
Esq., 1907 09 Lord High Commissioner to the Church of Scot-
land; 1914 K.T.; born 1847, succeeded his father, 1887, married
1875, Mary Alma Victoria, daughter of the late Sir Andrew
Agnew, Bart., and Lady Louisa Agnew, and has issue—Hon.
Catherine Mary, b. 1876, died 1886; Harry. b. and d. 1877;
Douglas Arthur, Master of Kinnaird, Captain Scots Guards
killed in action 1914, b. 1879; Kenneth Fitzgerald, Captain
in Scottish Horse, b. 1880 (m. 1903, Frances O. Clifton);
Noel-Andrew, b. and d 1883; Hon. Arthur Middleton, b. 1885,
A.D.C. to General Rycroft, Commanding 32nd Division,
killed in action 1917; Hon. Margaret Alma, b. 1892; Hon.
Patrick Charles, b. 1898.   Seats—Rossie Priory, Inchture,
Perthshire. London Residence—10 St. James's Square, S.W.1.

(GEORGE III., 1801)—JOHN CAMPBELL, BARON ABER-
CROMBY OF ABOUKIR and TULLIBODY, U.K., etc.,
son of George 3rd Lord, by Louisa Penuel Forbes, daughter
of the late Lord Medwyn, late Lieut. Rifle Brigade, is President
Society of Antiquaries of Scotland, born 1841; succeeded his
brother 1917; married 1876, Adele-Wilhelmine Marika (whom
he divorced 1879), only daughter of Charles von Herdenstam)
and has issue Edla Louise Montague, b 1877, m. 1906, Georges
H. Nasos. Athens. His Lordship has a sister, the Hon.
Montagu, born 1835 (married 1856, George Frederick, 6th Earl
of Glasgow, who died 1890). Seat—Tullibody. Clackmannanshire. Residence—62 Palmerston Place, Edinburgh.

LANSDOWNE MARQUIS OF, BARON NAIRNE, Henry-
Charles-Keith Petty-Fitzmaurice, 1681 Baron Nairne; in the
Peerage of Great Britain, 1760 Baron Wycombe of Chipping
Wycombe; 1784 Marquess of Lansdowne, Earl Wycombe, and
Viscount Calne and Calnstone; in the Peerage of Ireland,
1181 Baron of Kerry and Lixnaw; 1723 Earl of Kerry and
Viscount Clanmaurice; 1751 Viscount Fitzmaurice and Baron
of Dunkeron; 1753 Earl of Shelburne; 1883-88 Governor-
General of the Dominion of Canada; 1888-93 Viceroy and
Governor-General of India; 1884 G.C.M.G.; 1888 G.C.S.I. and
G.C.I.E.; 1894 K.G.; 1895 P.C. and Secretary of State for War
till 1900; Secy. of State for Foreign Affairs, 1900-1905;
Cabinet Minister, without portfolio, 1915-16; b. 1845; suc. his
father as 5th Marquess of Lansdowne 1886, and his mother
as Baron Nairne 1895; m. 1869 Lady Maud-Evelyn Hamilton,
daughter of James, 1st Duke of Abercorn K.G., and has issue—

1. Lady Evelyn-Emily-Mary b. 1870, m. 1892 the 9th Duke of Devonshire.

2. HENRY - WILLIAM - EDMOND, EARL OF KERRY, M.V.O, D.S.O., Lt.-Col. 2nd (Re-erve) Battn. Irish Guards b. 1872. m. 1904, Eliz beth Hope, and has issue—a daughter. b, 191 ; HENRY- MAURICE-JOHN, Viscount Calne and Calstone b. 1913.

3. Lord Charles-George-Francis, Mercer-Nairne, Major. 1st Royal Dragoons, born 1874; killed in action. 1914; married 1909 Lady Violet-Mary, 3rd daughter of the 4th Earl of Minto, and left issue. Lady Violet m. (2ndly) 1916 Capt the Hon. John Astor, 2nd son of 1st Viscount Astor.

4. Lady Beatrice-Frances, b. 1877, m. Marquis of Waterford.

His lordship's father, Henry, 4th Marquess of Lansdowne, 5th Earl of K rry, et ., K.G., was b. 1816; summoned to the House of Lords 1856, by his father's title of Baron Wycombe; suc. to the Marquessate 1863, and d. 1866, hav ng

m. 1st, 1840, Lady Georgina Herbert (d. 1841), daughter of George Augustus, 11th Earl of Pembroke, and 2ndly, 1843, the Hon. Emily Jane-Mercer-Elphinstone De Flahault (d 1895), in her own right Baroness Nairne, eldest daughter of the Comte de Flahault and the Baroness Nairne and Keith, and left issue by his second marriage—

1. The present peer.

2. Lord Edmond-George, now Lord Fitzmaurice, Barrister-at-Law, 1868-1885 M.P. for Calne, 1882-1885 Under Secretary of State for Foreign Affairs, 1906-8 Parliamentary Under Secy. for Foreign Affairs; 1908 Chancellor of the Duchy of Lancaster; b. 1846, m 1889 Caroline, daughter of W. J. Fitzgerald, Esq., of Litchfield, Connecticut, U.S., which marriage was annulled 1894.

3. Lady-Emily-Louisa-Ann, b. 1855, m. 1886 the Hon. Everard-Charles Digby, Colonel in the Army (who d. 1915), and has issue.

Seats—Bowood Park, Calne, Wilts; Derreen, Kenmare. co. Kerry. *London Residence.* 54 Berkeley Square, W.I.

(JAMES VI., 1607)—ALEXANDER HUGH BRUCE, 6TH BARON BALFOUR OF BURLEIGH, created 1607, attained 1715; relieved from attainder by Act of Parliament in 1869; 1872, Captain Highland Borderer Light Infantry Militia; 1882-9, chairman Educational Endowments (Scotland) Commission; 1892, a Privy Councillor; 1895-1903, Secretary for Scotland; 1901 K.T., and Chancellor of St. Andrew's University. 1909-10; G.C.M.G. 1911; G.C.V.O. 1917; Chairman of Royal Commission on Closer Trade Relations between Canada and the West Indies; born 1849, married Lady Catherine Eliza Gordon, youngest daughter of George John James, 5th Earl of Aberdeen (1876). and has issue— Hon. Mary, born 1877 (married 1910 Major John Augustus Hope. M.P.); Hon. Jane Hamilton. born 1879; Hon. Robert, Master of Burleigh, born 1880; Capt. A & S. Highlanders; killed in action, 1914; Hon. George-John-Gordon, born 1883, served in European War. Croix de Chevalier of Legion of Honour, 1917, married 1919 Violet Dorothy, daughter of R H. Done, Esq., Salterswell. Taporley, Cheshire; Hon. Victoria Alexandrina Katherine, born 1898. *Seat*— Kennet, Alloa. London Residence, 47 Cadogan Square. S.W.1.

ANCASTER, EARL OF, GILBERT HEATHCOTE DRUMMOND WILLOUGHBY. 1313, Baron Willoughby de Eresby in the Peerage of England; 1856, Baron Aveland, and in 1892, Earl of Ancaster, in the Peerage of the United Kingdom; 1732. a Baronet of England; M.P., for Horncastle Division of Lincolnshire, 1894-1910; Lt.-Col. Lincolnshire Yeomanry; born 1867; succeeded his father as 2nd Earl in 1910; married, 1905 Elvise, oldest daughter of the late W. L. Breese, Esq., New York, and

has issue—(1) Lady Catherine Mary Clementina, born 1906;
(2) Gilbert James, Lord Willoughby de Eresby, born 1907; (3)
Lady Priscilla, born 1909; Hon. John, born 1914. Seats—
Drummond Castle, Muthill, Perthshire; Grimsthorpe, Bourne,
Lincolnshire. London residence—Eresby Hall, Rutland Gate,
S.W.7.

DUNEDIN, BARON. ANDREW GRAHAM-MURRAY, created
1905 Baron Dunedin of Stenton in the county of Perth, M.A.
Cambridge, LL.D. Edinburgh, Glasgow. and Aberdeen, D.L.
Edinburgh, 1874 called to the Scottish Bar, 1890-1 Sheriff of
Perthshire, 1891 Q.C., 1891-1905 M.P. for Buteshire, 1891-2
and 1895-6 Solicitor-General for Scotland, 1896-1903 Lord
Advocate, 1896 Privy Councillor; 1900 Keeper of the Great
Seal of the Principality of Scotland, 1903-5 Secretary for Scot-
land and Vice-President of the Committee of Council on
Education for Scotland, with seat in the Cabinet; 1905-13 Lord
Justice-General and President of the Court of Session in Scotland;
1908 K.C.V.O.; 1913 a Lord of Appeal in Ordinary in
London; born 1849; married 1874, Mary Clementina, seventh
daughter of Admiral Sir Wm. Edmonstone, 4th Baronet, C.B.,
and has issue—(1) Hon. Ronald Thomas Graham, Captain 3rd
Batt. Black Watch, born 1875, married 1903, Evelyn, daughter of
the late Sir David Baird, 3rd bart.; (2) Hon. Mary Caroline, *d.*
1912; (3) Hon. Gladys Esme; (4) Hon. Marjorie, *m.* 1907 Capt. E.
L.C. Feilden, and has issue, Iris *b.* 1909. His Lordship's father
was Thos. Graham Murray of Stenton, Perthshire, LL.D., D.L.,.
Edinburgh, Writer to the Signet 1838, Crown Agent for Scot-
land 1866-8, third son of Andrew Graham Murray of Murrays-
hall, Sheriff of Aberdeenshire. Seat—Stenton, Dunkeld, N.B.
Town residence—7 Rothesay Terrace, Edinburgh. Clubs—
Carlton and Wellington, London; New Club and Scottish
Conservative. Edinburgh. London Address—20 Princes
Street, Hanover Square, W.1.

COURT OF LIEUTENANCY.

His Grace the Duke of Atholl, K.T., C.B., M.V.O., D.S.O.,
Lord-Lieutenant
Colonel Steuart Fothringham, Vice-Lieutenant
Mr David Marshall, solicitor, general clerk of Lieutenancy.

DEPUTY-LIEUTENANTS—PERTH.

Lord Provost of Perth	Col. Smythe of Methven	1893
Lord Ruthven of Gowrie 1866	The Earl of Mansfield	1912
Sir R. D. Moncreiffe, Bart. 1882		

Mr David Marshall, solicitor. clerk.

DUNKELD.

Col. Steuart Fothringham 1893	Major Blair Stewart	1912
Lord Forteviot 1912		

WEEM.

Major Stewart-Robertson 1901

CRIEFF.

R. T. N. Spier of Culdees 1890	Captain C. H. Graham Stirling	1901
Capt. W. A. H. Drummond Moray of Abercairney 1893	The Earl of Ancaster	1912

DUNBLANE.

Sir H. D. Erskine of Cardross 1879
Archibald Stirling of Keir 1893
John Stroyan, Lanrick 1905

Capt. Sir Malcolm MacGregor (of MacGregor), Bart. 1912

CARSE OF GOWRIE.

Lord Kinnaird 1872

Captain Malcolm Drummond of Megginch, 1893.

Mr David Marshall, clerk.

COUPAR-ANGUS.

Sir J. H. Ramsay, Bart. 1871

Colonel P. R. Burn Clerk Rattray 1912

CULROSS.

John James Dalgleish of West Grange, 1887

MEMBERS OF PARLIAMENT.

FOR THE COUNTY.

At the Union, when most of the shires in Scotland sent two members to the Scottish Parliament, Perth and ten other counties sent four.

Sir Patrick Murray of Ochtertyre, Bart., John Haldane of Gleneagles, Mungo Graham of Gorthy, and John Murray of Strowan, were the members for Perthshire.

1724 Dec. 31,......David Graham of Orchill unanimously elected
1726 April 28,....Mungo Haldane of Gleneagles ... } Candidates
    John Erskine of Balgownie ... }
    19 voted for Mr Haldane—14 for Mr Erskine
1727 Oct. 12.......J. Drummond of Megginch ... } Candidates
    Mungo Haldane of Gleneagles... }
    25 voted for Mr Drummond—14 for Mr Haldane
1734 May 9,........Lord John Murray unanimously elected
1741 May 21.......Lord John Murray   do
1747 July 10......Lord John Murray   do
1754 April 23,....Lord John Murray   do
1761 April 21,.....John Murray, Esq. of Strowan, unan. elected
1764 March 23....Col. David Græme of Gorthy, ... }
    George Drummond of Blair- } Candidates
    drummond ...   . }
    40 voted for Col. Græme—27 for Mr Drummond
1768 March 31,...Major-General D. Græme of Gorthy unanimously elected
1773 June 11,.....Col. James Murray of Strowan, } Candidates
    Thomas Graham of Balgowan, }
    48 voted for Col. Murray—42 for Mr Graham
1774 Nov. 11......Col. James Murray of Strowan, unan. elected
1780 Sept. 21,.....Col. James Murray of Strowan,   do
1784 April 15,....Maj.-Gen. Jas. Murray of Strowan, un. elected
1790 July 14,...Major-General James Murray of }
    Strowan, ... } Candidates
    John Drummond of Megginch, }
    67 voted for General Murray—38 for Mr Drummond
1794 April 11,....Lieut.-Col. T. Graham of Balgowan unanimously elected
1796 June 18,.....Col. Thos. Graham of Balgowan, unan. elected

1802 July 26,......Col. Thos. Graham of Balgowan, unan. elected
1806 Nov. 25, ...Col. Thos. Graham of Balgowan,   do
1807 May 19,......Lord James Murray.   do
1812 March 19,...James Drummond, Esq.,   ...
          Lieut.-Gen. Sir T. Graham of } Candidates
          Balgowan, K.B., ...
      69 voted for Mr Drummond—51 for Sir T. Graham
1812 Oct 26........James Drummond, Esq.,...   ...
          Lieut.-Gen. Sir T. Graham of } Candidates
          Balgowan, K.B.,   ...
      75 voted for Mr Drummond—68 for Sir T. Graham
1818 July 3,.......James Drummond, Esq., unanimously elected
1820 March 21,...James Drummond, Esq.,
1820 April 6, ...Major-General Sir George Murray of Drum-
          lanrig and Bleaton, unanimously elected
1826 June 10,.....Lieut.-General Sir Geo. Murray,   do
1828 June 16,.....Right Hon. Lt.-Gen. Sir G. Murray. do
1830 Aug. 29,.....Right Hon. Lt.-Gen. Sir G. Murray, do
1831 May 10,......Right Hon. Lt.-Gen. Sir G. Murray. do
1832 Dec. 27,......Earl of Ormelie, ... } Candidates
          Sir George Murray, ...
    1664 voted for Lord Ormelie—1090 for Sir George Murray
1834 May 2,........Sir George Murray, ... } Candidates
          R. Graham, Esq. of Redgorton,
    1464 voted for Sir George Murray - 1268 for Mr Graham
1835 Jan. 15,......Hon. Fox Maule. ...   . } Candidates
          Sir George Murray, ...
    1453 voted for Hon. Fox Maule—1371 for Sir George Murray
1837 Aug. 3, ...Viscount Stormont, ... } Candidates
          Hon. Fox Maule, ...
    1495 voted for Viscount Stormont—1379 for Hon. Fox Maule
1840 March 6,.....Mr Home Drummond, ... } Candidates
          Mr George D. Stewart, ...
    2586 voted for Mr Home Drummond—1128 for Mr George D.
          Stewart
1842 July 6,.......Mr Home Drummond unanimously elected
1847 Aug. 5,......Mr Home Drummond,   do
1852 July 16,......William Stirling, Esq. of Keir,   do
1857 March 28,...William Stirling, Esq. of Keir,   do
1859 May 2,.......William Stirling, Esq. of Keir,   do
1865 July 15,......Sir William Stirling-Maxwell, Bart. of Keir
          and Pollok, unanimously elected
1868 Nov. 21,......Mr C. S. Parker, ... } Candidates
          Sir Wm. Stirling-Maxwell, Bart. }
    2046 voted for Mr C. S. Parker—1767 for Sir W. S. Maxwell
1874 Feb. 11.......Sir Wm. Stirling-Maxwell, Bart., } Candidates
          Mr C. S. Parker, ...
    2554 voted for Sir W. S. Maxwell—2060 for C. S. Parker
1878 Feb. 2,........Henry Edward Stirling Home
          Drummond Moray, Captain
          and Lieutenant-Colonel, ... } Candidates
     Hon. Captain Algernon William
          Fulke Greville,
2439 voted for Colonel H. E. S. H. Drummond Moray—2255 for
      Hon. Captain Fulke Greville

1880 April 3,......Sir Donald Currie, K.C.M.G., ...⎫
Henry Edward Stirling Home ⎬ **Candidates**
Drummond Moray, Captain ⎪
and Lieutenant-Colonel ...⎭
Voted for Sir D. Currie, 2674 ; Colonel Moray, 2472---majority
for Sir D. Currie, 202
1885—First Election under the New Franchise Act
Western Perthshire, Sir D. Currie, 3786 ; Colonel Moray, 3290—
majority for Sir D. Currie, 496
Eastern Perthshire, R. S. Menzies, 4222 ; A. G. Murray, 2421--
majority for R. S. Menzies, 1801
1886 July 8, Western Perthshire, Sir D. Currie, 3269 ; Mr G. W.
S. Omond, 2329--majority, 940
1886 July 10, Eastern Perthshire. Mr R. S. Menzies, 3504 ; Mr
J. R, Holland, 2195—majority, 1309
1889 Feb. 19, Eastern Perthshire, Sir John Kinloch, 4005 ;
Mr W. L. Boase, 2289—majority, 1716
1892 July 12, Eastern Perthshire, Sir John Kinloch, 3533 ;
Mr W. L. Boase, 2484--majority, 1049
1892 July 8, Western Perthshire, Sir D. Currie, 3422 ; Mr. Alex.
Ure, 3053--majority, 369
1895 July 17, Western Perthshire, Sir D. Currie, 3379 ; Mr J.
D. Hope, 3087—majority, 292
1895 July 20, Eastern Perthshire, Sir John Kinloch, 3410 ; Mr
W. L. Boase, 2535--majority, 875
1900 October 6, Western Perthshire, Mr John Stroyan, 3598 ;
Mr C. S. Parker, 2913--majority, 685
1900 October 10, Eastern Perthshire, Sir John Kinloch, 3185 ;
Mr J. Graham Stewart, 2143—majority, 1042
1903 Feb. 26, Eastern Perthshire, T. R. Buchanan, unopposed.
1906 Jan. 19, Western Perthshire, Mr D. Erskine, 3890 ; Mr J.
Stroyan, 3087--majority, 803
„   „   23, Eastern Perthshire, Mr T. R. Buchanan, 3738 ;
Marquis of Tullibardine, 2648—majority, 1090
1910 Jan. 20, Western Perthshire, Marquis of Tullibardine,
3864 ; T. B. Morison, 3566—majority, 298.
1910 Jan. 25, Eastern Perthshire, William Young, 3884 ; Hon.
A. D. Murray, 2703--majority, 1181.
1910 December 8, Western Perthshire, Marquis of Tullibandine,
4027 ; G. F. Barbour, 3637—majority, 390.
1910 December 13, Eastern Perthshire, William Young, 3658 ;
A. N. Skelton, 2826—majority, 832.
1917 February, Western Perthshire, Col. Archibald Stirling—
unopposed.
1918—First Election under the Representation of the People
Act, 1918--
Kinross and Western Perthshire, James Gardiner, 7579 ;
Brig.-Gen. Arch. Stirling, 6975—majority, 604.
Perth Division, William Young—unopposed.

Agents for Kinross and Western Division—
Unionist—Malcolm Finlayson, Crieff.
Liberal—A. C. Campbell, Perth.

Agents for Perth Division—

Unionist—Alexander Stewart, Perth.
Liberal—W. Munro, Perth.

Number of Voters in Kinross and Western Division, 1919, ...23,148
Number of Voters in Perth Division, 1919, ... 37,795

MEMBERS OF PARLIAMENT FOR THE CITY.

1830 Dec. 24......L. Oliphant, Esq. of Condie.......⎱ Candidates
          Lord James Stuart....................⎰
    458 voted for Mr Oliphant—205 for Lord James Stuart
1834 Jan. 13......L. Oliphant, Esq,, elected without opposition
1837 July 26......Hon. Arthur Kinnaird.............⎱ Candidates
          Sir P. Murray Threipland.........⎰
    355 voted for Hon. A. Kinnaird—188 for Sir P. M. Threipland
1839 Aug. 19......David Greig Esq., Lord Provost, elected with-
          out opposition.
1841 July 8.......The Right Hon. Fox Maule........⎱ Candidates
          Mr W. F. Black.........⎰
    356 voted for Right Hon. Fox Maule—227 for Mr W. F. Black
1846 July 11......Right Hon. Fox Maule, unanimously elected
1847 July 30......Right Hon. Fox Maule,   do
1852 Feb. 8 ......Right Hon. Fox Maule,   do
1852 May 14......Hon. Arthur Kinnaird..............⎱ Candidates
          Mr Charles Gilpin...................,⎰
    325 voted for Hon. Arthur Kinnaird—225 for Mr Gilpin
1852 July 9........Hon. Arthur Kinnaird, unanimously elected
1857 March 28...Hon. Arthur Kinnaird,   do
1859 April 28.....Hon. Arthur Kinnaird,   do
1865 July 11......Hon. Arthur Kinnaird,   do
1868 Nov. 17......Hon. Arthur Kinnaird,   do
1874 Feb. 4.......Hon. Arthur Kinnaird..............⎱ Candidates
          Mr Charles Scott, advocate ....⎰
    1648 voted for Hon. Arthur Kinnaird—940 for Mr Charles Scott
1877 Jan. 29......Mr C. S. Parker.........................⎱ Candidates
          Dr Mackie................................⎰
    2206 voted for Mr C. S. Parker—855 for Dr Mackie
1880 April 1......Mr C. S. Parker ....⎱ Candidates
          Colonel Williamson ....⎰
    Mr Parker, 2315; Colonel Williamson, 774—majority, 1541
1885 Nov. 24......Mr C. S. Parker.....................,......⎱
          Mr J. Chisholm..........................⎬Candidates
          Mr A. M'Dougall, jun. ....⎰
Mr Parker, 1652; Mr Chisholm, 1099; Mr M'Dougall, 967—
          majority, 553

1886 July 2.......Mr C. S. Parker, 1573; Mr W. Fowler, 1120--
        majority, 453
1892 July 5 ......Mr W. Whitelaw.........................⎫
         Mr C. S. Parker.......................⎬ Candidates
         Mr Jas. Woollen.....................⎭
   Mr Whitelaw, 1398; Mr Parker, 1171; Mr Woollen, 907
1895 July 13......Mr R. Wallace.................................2137
         Mr W. Whitelaw.............................1763
         Majority,.............. 374
1900 October 2...Mr R. Wallace.................................2171
         Mr W. Whitelaw............................1827
         Majority,.............. 344
1906 Jan. 13......Mr R. Wallace,................................2875
         Mr S. Chapman,.............................1867
         Majority,................1008
1907 Jan. 13......Sir Robert Pullar, unopposed.
1910 Jan. 17......Mr. A. F. Whyte,..............................2841
         Mr. S. Chapman,...........................2103
         Majority,.............. 738
1910 Dec. 3......Mr. A. F. Whyte,.............. 2852
         Colonel Telfer-Smollett.....................1878
         Majority,. 974
  Under the Representation of the People Act, 1918. Perth City
is now included in Perth Division.

JUSTICES OF THE PEACE.

*No Justice can legally act who has not qualified by subscrib-
ing the Statutory Oaths in the Register kept by the Clerk of the
Peace in Perth.*

Duke of Atholl, K.T., C.B.,
  M.V.O., D.S.O.
Duchess of Atholl, LL.D.
Duke of Montrose, K.T.
Marquis of Breadalbane, K.G.
Earl of Mansfield
Earl of Moray
Earl of Ancaster
Viscount Haldane, K.T.
Lord Rollo
Lord Kinnaird, K.T.
Lord Dunedin of Stenton
Lord Forteviot, Dupplin
  Castle.
Hon. Alex. D. Murray, of
  Pitfour
Sir J.H. Ramsay of Bamff, Bart.
Sir Patrick Keith Murray of
  Ochtertyre, Bart.
Sir Robert Drummond Mon-
  creiffe of Moncreiffe, Bart.
Sir Alexander Kay Muir, Bart.,
  of Blairdrummond, Doune.

Sir Wm. Dunbar, Bart., Earn-
  bank, Bridge of Earn
Sir George W. M. Dundas of
  Dunira, Bart.
Sir George Kinloch of Kin-
  loch, Bart.
Sir Malcolm MacGregor, Bart.,
  R.N., Edinchip
Sir Henry David Erskine of
  Cardross, M.V.O.
Sir Wm Stowell Haldane, W.S.,
  of Foswell, Auchterarder
John Alexander, butcher
  Alyth
Archibald Adie, Crieff
Peter Anderson, Fortingall
Alexander H. Anderson, Dun-
  blane
Frank Balfour of Kindrogan
Geo. Freeland Barbour of Bon-
  skeid
James Barlas, house factor,
  Perth .
Wm. Baxter, Tophead, Stanley

Geo. Bell, Inchmichael, Errol

Alex. W. Bennet, bank agent, Blairgowrie

George S. Bisset, implement maker, Rattray

R. Robertson Black, Blairgowrie

John L. Bowie, Solicitor, Perth

Chas. Boyd, banker, Co.-Angus

Robert Brough, Bridge of Earn

P. Brown, Devon Cottage, Stanley

Andrew Bruce, farmer, Jordanstone, Meigle

William Brydie, farmer, Shielhill, Braco

Wm. Brown, Kirkton, Trinity Gask

Charles A. Butter of Cluniemore, Pitlochry

John Butter, Kirkhill. Meigle

T. Buttar, Corston. Co.-Angus

John Hamilton Buchanan of Leny, Callander

Archibald Cameron, Kinloch Rannoch

Robert W. G. Cameron, of Drumharrie, Gask

Colonel John C. Campbell of Achalader

Brigadier-General John H. Campbell, of Inverardoch

Alexander Campbell, Boreland, Fernan

Duncan Campbell, farm manager, Balnacraig, Fortingall

H. Campbell, banker, Crieff

Bailie John Campbell, Edron House, Feus Road, Perth

John Joseph Calder, Ardargie House, Forgandenny

Peter Carmichael, farmer, Kirklands, Aberuthven

J. Carmichael of Arthurstone

D. C. R. Lindsay Carnegie of Ashintully and Glendevon

James Carnegie of Stronvar

James Chalmers, draper, Coupar Angus

Charles Chick, Union Bank, Dunblane

John Clark, manager, Co-operative Society, Perth

George Clayton, manufacturer, Glendevon

Col. W. Clark of Princeland Coupar-Angus

Lt.-Col. Charles E. Colville, O.B.E., solicitor, Crieff

Peter Comrie, Drummie, Crieff

Robert Riddell Constable, of Cally

Albert Edward Cox of Dungarthill, Dunkeld

Alfred W. Cox of Glendoick, Kinfauns

William Henry Cox of Snaigow, Dunkeld

George Crabbie of Blairhoyle, Port of Monteith

Rev. Thomas Crawford, of Orchill

Nickel Crombie, Perth

James Cuthbert, Perth

William B. Dickie, of Whitehills, Inchture

Captain the Hon. John Dewar, M.C., Dupplin Castle, Perth

David G. Donaldson M.D., Dunning

James Duff, farmer, Inveredrie, Glenshee

Arthur Hay Drummond of Cromlix, Dunblane

Captain Malcolm Drummond of Megginch

Miss Mary Drummond, Mains of Megginch, Errol

David Donald, builder, Braeside, New Scone

S. Drysdale, Solicitor, Crieff

William Ellison, Craigville, Perth

George Turnbull Ewing, Pitkellony, Muthill

John S. Fairweather, merchant, Meigle

Miss Mary M. Fairweather, The Elms, Meigle

William Fenton, upholsterer, Pitlochry

Robert Fergusson, farmer Muirlaggan, Balquhidder.

Donald Stewart Fergusson Dunfallandy

Andrew M. Ferguson, solicitor, Alyth

Alexander Fergusson, farmer, Netherton of Dalcapon, Ballinluig

Col. Walter T. J. S. Steuart Fothringham of Grandtully

John M. Fraser of Invermay

Wm. E. Frost, Ardvreck, Crieff

Thomas Jackson Gardiner, farmer, Banchory, Coupar Angus

James Gardiner, M.P., Dargill, Crieff

Major Lewis Gibson, Union Bank, Perth

Rev Wm. Alexander Gillies, The Manse, Kenmore

James J. Gillespie, Briarbank Glasgow Road, Perth

A. G. Maxtone Graham of Cultoquhey

Alex. Graham, farmer, Hill, Errol

John Graham, farmer, Tippermallo

A. M. B. Grahame of Arntomy, Port of Monteith

Major John P. Grant, of Kilgraston

George Gordon, ironmonger, Alyth

Ernest Hry. Graham-Stirling, Camp Cottage, Comrie

Alex. Price Haig of Blair-Hill

Miss Haldane, Cloan, Auchterarder

J.G. Hay Halkett of Balendoch

Robert F. Hally, manufacturer, Auchterarder

Robert Halley, Perth

Daniel Hardie, Crieff

Lt.-Col. J. A. G. Drummond Hay, Seggieden

Wm. Henderson, Lawton, Coupar-Angus

James M. Hodge, solicitor, Blairgowrie

William C. Hunter, W.S., of Arngask

Stuart Honeyman, Blairgowrie

Thomas. Hunter, editor *Perthshire Constitutional*. Perth

Robert Inglis, factor, Old Blair

John Irvine, M.D., Muthill

Rev. James William Jack, U.F. Manse, Glenfarg

Henry William Johnston, Dunross, Strathtay

Alex. Johnston, M.D., Methven

Thomas N. Johnstone, farmer, Malling, Port of Monteith

Pat. Leslie Johnston, merchant, Templehall, Longforgan

James Peebles Kennaway, solicitor, Auchterarder

Robert M. Kippen, solicitor, Perth

Robert Keay, City Chamberlain, Perth

Alex. Kerr, cabinetm'ker, Crieff

James Kidd, farmer, Mains of Errol

C. Young Kinloch, of Gourdie

Robert Lambie, merchant, Crianlarich

M. H. Lawson, banker, Dunning

John Gibson Leitch, M.D., of Wester Boquhapple, Thornhill.

John Lowe, M.B.C.M., Coupar-Angus

John L. Low, late of Butterstone. Taypark, Dundee

David Loudon, grocer, Barbeth, Queen's Avenue, Perth

R. O. Lumsden, farmer, Pitcairnfield, Perth

Alex. P. Lyle, of Glendelvine

James M'Anish, Balkerack Street, Doune

Alexander M'Beth, retired bank agent, Pitlochry

Alexander M'Donald, factor, Meggernie

Duncan M'Donald, blacksmith Kinloch Rannoch

Thomas M'Donald, draper, Callander

Alex. M'Diarmid, Rotmell Ballinluig

James M'Duff of Tomnagrew, Strathbraan

Alex. Macduff of Bonhard

Daniel M'Farlane, Gartmore, Port of Monteith

J. Macfee, surgeon, Auchterarder

Atholl M'Gregor, Ard-choille, Perth

Thomas M'Gregor, farmer, Millbank, Meikleour

William M'Gregor, farmer, Newbigging

Robert M'Gillewie, banker, Dunkeld

Peter M'Intyre, Hillbrook, Strathyre

W. A. M'Intyre, Erichtside, Blairgowrie

Peter M'Intyre, Tignablair, Comrie

John Mackay, M.D., Aberfeldy

Robert W. R. Mackenzie, Earlshall

Chas. M'Kenzie of Borland

Donald M'Kenzie, Banker, Perth

Duncan MacNab, solicitor, Perth

John M'Naughton of Inver-lochlarig, Balquhidder

Robert M'Naughtan of Cowden

John M'Nee, Crieff

William C Macpherson, Blairgowrie

Peter M'Pherson, merchant, Comrie

James Davidson M'Rae, auctioneer, Killin

John Main, draper, Doune

James Mair, Aberfoyle

H. Martin, Flowerdale, Collace

Donald M'Dougall, farmer, Dall, Ardeonaig, Loch Tay

Thomas M'Glashan, M.A., teacher, Killiecrankie

Angus M'Gregor, postmaster, Butterstone

Andrew Macfarlane, farmer, Netherton, Blackford

James M. Marshall, Bleaton Hallet, Blairgowrie

John M. Matthew, Auchmague, Perth

Sydney George Meacher, surveyor, Marlee House, by Blairgowrie

James Melrose, Kirkton, Aberfoyle

William Dudgeon Graham Menzies of Hallyburton

H. Mitchell, banker, Pitlochry

George Mitchell, wood turner, Knap, Longforgan

Arch. Miller, coachbuilder, Crieff

Francis Norie Miller, of Cleeve, Perth

George A. Miller, W.S., Perth

R. Hoyer Miller of Blair Castle, Culross

John B Miller, solicitor, Blairgowrie

Captain M. M. Moncrieff, of Bandirran.

Robt. Morris, potato merchant, Burrelton

Guy E. Broun-Morison, of Finderlie and Murie

Thos. B. Morison, K.C., Comrie

Wm. Morison, Newmiln, Perth

Robert A. Mossman, M.D., Kinloch Rannoch

Captain W. A. H. Drummond Moray of Abercairny

C. Munro, banker, Aberfeldy

William Murray, Chapelhill, Methven

John Murray, Dunblane

J. F. Murray, Leitfie, Alyth

D. Keith Murray, Kondoli, Crieff

Donald M'Laren, farmer, Bracklinn, Callander

Charles A. Murray, Taymount

Wm. Watson Murray, Catter House, Drymen

Provost John Stewart M'Culloch, watchmaker, Auchterarder

James M'Ara, nurseryman, Galvelbeg. Crieff

Captain James MacRosty, banker, Crieff

Rev. Hotchkin Haynes Murray, Manse of Monzie, Crieff

Archibald John Percy Murray, Logie House, Methven

Robt. Peter M'Lagan, farmer, East Mid Lamberkin, Aberdalgie

John M'Leish, farmer, Wester Cairnie, Forteviot, Forgandenny

Thomas Myles, farmer, Montague, Scone

Duncan M'Ewan, farmer, Over Kinfauns, by Perth

Rev.Coll. Archibald M'Donald, C.F., The Manse, Logierait

Andrew M'Gregor Meldrum, solicitor, Pitlochry

William Niven, farmer, Loan of Errol, Errol

Alex. Cecil Newbigging of Dalchonzie

Norm. J. Nasmyth of Glenfarg

Charles James George Paterson of Castle Huntly

Robert Paterson, Hill of Drip, by Stirling

John Paterson, farmer, Kirkton, Tyndrum

James Paton, farmer, Obney

James Playfair of Isla Bank

Alex. Moncur Prain, Edinburgh

Henry Prain, farmer, Helenbank, Longforgan

John Prain, Invergowrie

R. C. Campbell Preston (late of Valleyfield), Ardchattan

George Pitcaithly, farmer, West Dron, Bridge of Earn

Neil Paton, watchmaker 7 St., John Street, Perth

Albert E. Pullar, The Durn Perth

Herbert S. Pullar, Dunbarney,

Captain James Douglas Ramsay, yr. of Bamff, Alyth

Thos. Wilkie Reid, sub-postmaster, Methven

Col. Paul Burn Clerk-Rattray, of Craighall, Rattray

James M. Rae H. Robertson, Bridge of Earn

Andrew Thomson Reid, Auchterarder House

Alex. Reid, farmer, The Garth, Blairgowrie

Ernest F. Robertson of Auchleeks

J. Stewart Robertson of Edradynate

Peter S. Robertson, Merchant, Blairgowrie

Jas. Rodger, factor, Dunblane

James Arthur Rollo, Perth

Walter N. Russell, Glendevon, Dollar

James Stewart, sheep farmer, Clachan, Struan

Provost David Alexander Sandilands, draper, Logie Park, Alyth

James R. Sharp, Viewfield, Blackford

Thomas Redpath Scott Sibbald, M.D., Stanley

Gavin Strang, farmer, Moneydie, by Perth

Charles Scott, O.B.E., ex-Lord Provost of Perth

James Simpson, miller, Northbank, Perth

Edward Smart, rector, Perth Academy, Perth

Alex. Scott, Callander

J. Scott, Eastertyre, Logierait

Jas. Scott, Logierait Mill

Col. D. M. Smythe of Methven

Mrs. Barbara Ross Smythe, O.B.E., Clyde Place, Perth.

John F. Smith, Eastfield, Bridge of Earn

George Keddie Smith, Ballomill, Abernethy

Henry Smith, baker, Pitlochry

James Speid, Forneth

Robert T. N. Speir of Culdees

John Stewart, Mains of Downie, Strathardle

John G. Stewart, Aultwharrie, Dunblane

Peter Stewart, Killin

Major Alex. B. Stewart of Balnakeilly

Captain John M. S. Steuart, Strathtay

Alexander Stewart of Innerhadden, Washington, U.S.A.

Hinton Daniel Stewart of Strathgarry

Charles Murray Stewart, Kinachoile, Dunblane

Brig.-Gen. Arch. Stirling of Keir

The Honble. Mrs. Margaret M. Stirling, Keir, Dunblane

Major C. H. G. Stirling of Strowan
J. Stroyan of Lanrick, Doune
Bailie Jas. Tainsh, plasterer, Strathearn View, Crieff
George Tasker, farmer, Arnbog, Meigle
James M. Taylor, shoemaker, Blackford
Jas. Taylor, 22 James St., Perth
David Templeman, Ex-Provost, Blairgowrie
Frank Lewis de Sales La Terriere. Dunalastair
Andrew Thomson, Edinburgh
And. Thomson, Astral Villa, Muckhart
Thomas Thomson, mill spinner, Bramble Bank House, Rattray
James Thom, farmer, Cambusmichael, Guildtown
Captain Wm. Murray Thriepland of Fingask
William Walker, farmer. The Rawes, Longforgan
William Whitson of Isla Park, Coupar-Angus
James Cairns Wright. Dunblane
John Moncrieff Wright, of Kinmonth, Bridge of Earn
Martin Henry Pirie Watt, bank agent, Crieff
John Yeaman, banker, Meigle
Thomas Young, Newbigging, Methven
Robert Young, builder, Viewfield House, Bankfoot

And for the time being —

The Sheriff of the County of Perth and his Substitutes.
The Sheriffs and Sheriff-Substitutes of the Counties of Forfar, Fife, Kinross, and Clackmannan.
The Convener of the County of Perth.
The Chairman of each District Committee of County Council.
The first or principal Magistrate of the Royal Burgh of Perth.
The Dean of Guild of the Royal Burgh of Perth.
The two senior Bailies of the Royal Burgh of Perth.
The Baron Bailies of Dunkeld and Blairgowrie.
The Senior Magistrates of Auchterarder, Coupar-Angus, Crieff, Dunblane, Abernethy, Alyth, Blairgowrie, Rattray, Callander, Aberfeldy, Doune.
The Chairman of each Parish Council.

Alexander Stewart, solicitor, Perth, Clerk of the Peace.
David M. Mackay, solicitor, Perth, Depute Clerk of the Peace.
Office: —31 George Street, Perth.

QUARTER SESSIONS.

The Statutory Quarter Sessions of Justices are—

First Tuesday of March	First Tuesday of August
First Tuesday of May	Last Tuesday of October

With adjournments when required.

COUNTY LICENSING APPEAL COURT

Consists of fourteen members —seven elected by the County Council, and seven by the Justices of the Peace.

PERTH BURGH LICENSING APPEAL COURT.

Consists of the six Magistrates of the Burgh, and six Justices appointed by the Justices of the Peace.

MEETINGS OF DISTRICT LICENSING COURTS.

WINES AND SPIRITS, PORTER, ALE, ETC.

Third Tuesday of April and last Tuesday of October in the several districts. Applications for Licenses must be lodged, according to printed forms (to be had of the District Clerks of the Peace), with the district clerks fourteen days before the meeting; and appeals and applications for confirmation must be lodged with the Clerk of the Peace, Perth, within ten days after the District Courts.

County Licensing Appeal Court for appeals and confirmations meets at Perth on the third Tuesday after the District Licensing Courts in April, and on the third Monday after the District Courts in October.

Burgh of Perth Licensing Appeal Court on third Tuesday after the Burgh Licensing Courts.

DISTRICTS OF COUNTY LICENSING COURTS AND JUSTICE OF PEACE COURTS.

The County of Perth is divided into five different districts, viz.

I. PERTH DISTRICT.

Parishes of Aberdalgie, Abernethy, Abernyte, Arngask, Auchtergaven, Dron, Dunbarney, Errol, Findo-Fask, Forgandenny, Forteviot, Inchture, Kilspindie, Kinclaven, Kinfauns, Kinnaird, Kinnoull, Longforgan, Methven, Moneydie, Perth (excluding the Burgh thereof), Redgorton, Rhynd, St. Madoes, Scone, Tibbermuir

Place of meeting, Perth. Alexander Stewart, solicitor Clerk of the Peace.

II. BLAIRGOWRIE OR EASTERN DISTRICT.

Parishes of Alyth, Bendochy, Blairgowrie, Caputh, Cargill, Clunie, Collace, Coupar-Angus, Kinloch, Kirkmichael, Lethendy, Meigle, Rattray, St. Martins.

Places of meeting—Blairgowrie for April Court, and Coupar Angus for October Court.

Charles Boyd, solicitor, Coupar-Angus, Depute-Clerk

III. CENTRAL DISTRICT.

Parishes of Auchterarder, Blackford, Comrie, Crieff, Dunning, Fowlis-Wester, Glendevon, Logiealmond, Madderty, Monzievaird and Strowan; Muckhart, Muthill, Trinity-Gask.

Place of meeting, Crieff. James P. Kennaway, Solicitor Auchterarder, Depute-Clerk.

IV. WESTERN DISTRICT.

Parishes of Aberfoyle, Ardoch, Balquhidder, Callander, Dunblane, Kilmadock, Killin, Kincardine, Lecropt, Port of Monteith.

Place of meeting, Dunblane. John Stewart, solicitor, Dunblane, Depute-Clerk.

V. HIGHLAND DISTRICT.

Parishes of Blair-Atholl, Dull, Dunkeld and Dowally, Fortingall, Kenmore, Little Dunkeld, Logierait, Moulin, Weem.

Place of Meeting, Logierait. C. H. Gordon, solicitor, Pitlochry, Depute-Clerk.

N.B.—The division of the County is applicable only to statutory duties. The ordinary jurisdiction of Justices extends over he whole County.

DEALERS IN GAME.

Under 1 and 2 Will. IV., cap. 32, and 23 and 24 Vict., cap. 90, and previous relative Acts, Licenses to persons to deal in game may be granted at any time during the year; but the yearly licensing meetings of Justices in the districts are held on the first lawful day in July.

SHERIFFS OF PERTHSHIRE.

1748 James Erskine, afterwards Lord Alva
- 54 John Swinton,   „   Lord Swinton
- 83 William Nairne,   „   Lord Dunsinane
- 83 David Smythe,   „   Lord Methven
- 93 Archibald Campbell Colquhoun of Clathick, afterwards Lord Clerk Register
- 1807 John Hay Forbes, afterwards Lord Medwyn (died 1854)
- 24 Duncan M'Neill, afterwards Lord Justice-General, and Lord Colonsay, in the House of Lords (died 1874)
- 35 Adam Anderson, afterwards Lord Anderson (died 1853)
- 1843 Robert Whigham (died 1849)
- 49 James Crauford, afterwards Lord Ardmillan (died 1876)
- 53 David Mure, afterwards Solicitor-General, Lord Advocate, and M.P. for Bute, afterwards Lord Mure
- 58 Edward S. Gordon, Q.C., afterwards Solicitor-General and Lord Advocate; M.P. for Universities of Glasgow and Aberdeen (1869); called to the House of Lords as Lord Gordon of Drumearn; (died 1879)
- 66 John Tait, formerly Sheriff of Kinross, Clackmannan and Linlithgow (resigned 1874; died 1877)
- 74 James Adam, Advocate, appointed Judge of Session and Justiciary (1877), afterwards Lord Adam (dead)
- 77 Robert Lee, formerly Sheriff of Stirling and Dumbarton, afterwards Lord Lee (dead)
- 80 John Hay Athol Macdonald, afterwards Lord-Justice-Clerk (dead).
- 85 Wm. Ellis Gloag, afterwards Lord Kincairney (died 1909).
- 89 Sir Chas. J. Pearson, afterwards Lord Pearson (died 1909)

90 Andrew Graham Murray, K.C., now Baron Dunedin of Stenton ; 1913, a Lord of Appeal in ordinary in London

91 And. Jameson. K C., afterwards Lord Ardwall (died 1911)

1905 Christopher N. Johnston, K.C., now Lord Sands.

1917 John Wilson, K.C., now Lord Ashmore

1920 J. C. S. Sandeman, K.C.

SHERIFF-SUBSTITUTES.

Perth.

1748 {	John Richardson	1833-83	Hugh Barclay (removed from Dunblane)
	George Miller		
69	William Mercer	83	John Grahame (d. 1899)
85	Patrick Duncan, senior	99	John David Sym
90	James Chalmers	1920	Claud Patrick Boswell
1808	Charles Husband		

Dunblane.

1748	Robert Campbell	1833	W. Hansom Colquhoun (appointed to Inverness)
55	Thomas Duthie		
74	George Menzies	36	John Pitcairn Trotter (appointed to Dumfries) (died 1867)
89	John Coldstream		
1825	George Bailie		
29	Hugh Barclay (appointed to Perth in 1833)	39	Andrew Cross (died 1857)
		57	John Graham d. 1899)

Killin.

1748 D. Campbell of Glenure | 1764 J. Campbell, Lochdochart. Abolished in 1770.

SHERIFF COURT.

The Sheriffdom of Perthshire is divided into two districts—First, Perth District, comprehending the following parishes, viz.:—Perth, Forgandenny, Dron, Arngask, Abernethy, Dunbarney, Rhynd, Aberdalgie, Forteviot, Dunning, Glendevon, Tibbermore, Findo-Gask, Trinity-Gask, Auchterarder, Blackford, Methven, Madderty, Muthill, Crieff, Monzievaird, Comrie, Logiealmond, Logierait, Scone, St. Martins, Cargill. Kinclaven, Fowlis-Wester, Redgorton, Moneydie, Auchtergaven, Dunkeld, Little Dunkeld, Kirkmichael, Moulin, Blair-Atholl, Fortingall, part of Kenmore, Dull, part of Weem, Caputh, Lethendy, Cluny, Kinloch, Blairgowrie, Rattray, Alyth, Meigle, Coupar-Angus, Bendochy, Collace, Kinnoull, Kinfauns, St. Madoes, Errol, Inchture, Lonforgan, Fowlis-Easter, Abernyte, Kinnaird, and Kilspindie. Where defenders reside in different districts the action must be brought in the Perth Court. This

Court is held at Perth every Tuesday and Friday during the session, and one Court, at least, is held in each vacation.

Condie Sandeman, K.C. (1920)
Claud Patrick Boswell, L.L.B., advocate, Sheriff Substitute (1920)
John Ritchie, Sheriff-Clerk (1914)
John Dickson, Depute-Clerk (1892)
John Robertson, do.   do   (1903)
Martin L. Howman, Procurator-Fiscal (1915)
John Dickson, Auditor of Law Accounts (1905)
J. G. Cran, Bar Officer (1906)
James Murray, Librarian (1911)

Poor's Agents—For Perth District, George Purvis, Alan Hunter, and J. C. Cameron; for Crieff, S. Graham Mickel; for Auchterarder, John Macfarlane; for Blairgowrie, Alyth, and Coupar-Angus, John Stewart; for Aberfeldy and Pitlochry Districts, Andrew Clow; Carse District, C. P. Campbell.

Accountants—J. & R. Morison, Blackfriars St.; Moir, Wood & Co., Royal Bank Buildings; J. Maxtone Graham, C.A., Clydesdale Bank Buildings; P. Nisbet, C.A., Clydesdale Bank Buildings.

Second or Dunblane District, comprehending the following parishes, viz.:—Dunblane, Callander, Balquhidder, Aberfoyle, Kincardine, Kilmadock, Lecropt, Port, Kippen, Killin, and Muckhart. Those portions of the parish of Kenmore, which lie to the west of the burn of Auldvine, on the south side of Loch Tay, and the burn of Lawers on the north side of Loch Tay, with a straight line across Loch Tay from the mouth of the former burn to the mouth of the latter burn. The portions of the parish of Weem, lying to the west of the said burn of Auldvine and Lawers, excepting the portions of the said parish situated in Glenlyon, and that part of the parish of Comrie be-west the east end of Lochearn, and those parts of the parishes of Muthill and Blackford lying be-south the Muir of Orchill. This Court is held at Dunblane every Wednesday of the session.

Note.—The other Parishes and parts of Parishes not included in the above, and attached to the Courts of Perth and Dunblane, continue so attached—that portion of the Parish of Blackford north of the road leading from the Roman Camp at Ardoch to Auchterarder being attached to Perth, and that portion to the south of the said road being attached to the Court of Dunblane.

Power is given by the statute, on cause shown to endorse cases from one District Court to another.

Claud Patrick Boswell, L.L.B., Sheriff Substitute of Perthshire.

Alexander M'Gillivray, Sheriff-Clerk Depute.

Alexander M'Gillivray, auditor.

R. Richardson, Sheriff and Bar officer.

The following statutory terms of session are observed in Sheriff Courts:—Each Sheriff holds two Sessions in each year called the Winter and Summer Session. The Winter Session commences on the 1st October, or the first Court Day thereafter, and ends on the last Court Day in March, with a recess at Christmas not exceeding Fifteen days. The Summer Session commences on the 1st day of May, or the first Court Day thereafter, and ends on the last Court Day in July; but one Court at least must be held in the Spring vacation, and two Courts at least in the Autumn vacation.

SHERIFF'S SMALL-DEBT COURTS.

The Sheriff holds a Circuit Court for Small-Debt causes—
At Blairgowrie on the Second Saturday of January and First Saturday of April, July, and October. J. B. Miller, Blairgowrie, Depute-Clerk. This Court has jurisdiction over the Parishes of Rattray, Kinloch, Kirkmichael, Blairgowrie, Alyth, Bendochy, Coupar-Angus, Meigle, Lethendy, and Clunie,

SHERIFF OFFICERS.

Perth	A. A. Hutton
	J. G. Cran (Bar Officer)
Dunblane	R. Richardson (Bar Officer)
Blairgowrie	John Mailer

MESSENGER-AT-ARMS.

Perth......A. A. Hutton.

COUNTY COUNCIL OF THE COUNTY OF PERTH
1919-1922,

as at December, 1919.

Convener—The Earl of Mansfield
Vice-Convener—Wm. Henderson, Esq.

I.—PERTH DISTRICT

N. J. Nasmyth, Glenf'rg House
John F. Smith, Eastfield
Lord Forteviot Dupplin
Geo. Pople, Newhouse, Perth
Col. Smythe of Methven
Charles A Murray, Taymount
Rev. A. M. Wyllie. Manse, Auchtergaven
James Fenwick. Kirkhill
Alexander Macduff, Bonhard

Charles Hutchison, Scone
The Earl of Moray, Kinfauns Castle
Thomas Hollingworth, Newmains, Inchture
Vacant
Arch. Powrie, Dialfield, Abernethy
David Hardie, Errol Estates Office, Errol

II.--BLAIRGOWRIE OR EASTERN DISTRICT

.J. M. Matthew, Auchmague
William Henderson, Lawton
Geo. Tasker, Arnbog, Meigle
.Sir James Henry Ramsay, Bart. of Bamff
.James M. Hodge, Old Rattray
R. R. Constable, Corriefodly
W. H. Cox of Snaigow

A. M. Ferguson, Alyth
W. C. Macpherson, Blairgowrie House, Blairgowrie
Charles Boyd, solicitor, Coupar-Angus
Andrew Spalding, 3 Leslie Street, Blairgowrie
Col. P. R. Burn Clerk Rattray. of Craighall

III.--HIGHLAND DISTRICT

The Duke of Atholl, K.T,.C,B., M.V.O., D.S.O., Blair Castle
·Colonel Steuart Fothringham, Murthly Castle
D. Stewart Fergusson, Dunfallandy, Pitlochry
.J. Stewart Robertson of Edradynate
The Marquis of Breadalbane, K.G., Taymouth Castle, Aberfeldy

A. Macdonald, Meggernie
Capt. F. de Sales La Terriere of Dunalastair
Robert Inglis, Old Blair
William Fenton, Pitlochry
Major Blair-Stewart of Balnakeilly, Pitlochry
A. Clow, Aberfeldy

IV.--CENTRAL DISTRICT

.John P. Mitchell, solicitor, Comrie
Major C. Home Graham Stirling of Strowan.
The Earl of Mansfield, Scone Palace
.A. Gregor Dixon, of Glentulchan, Glenalmond
·G. T. Ewing, Pitkellony, Muthill
W. Cairns, Dalchruim, Comrie

James P. Kennaway, solicitor' Auchterarder
William Gardiner, Henhill, Auchterarder
Lord Rollo, Duncrub House, Dunning
Andrew Thomson, Astral Villa, Muckhart, Dollar
John M'Nee, preserve manufacturer, Crieff
W. A. Dron, Crieffvechter, Crieff

V.--WESTERN DISTRICT

Campbell Willison, Killin
Donald M'Laren, Brackland, Callander
Wm. W. Murray, Catter House
:Sir A. Kay Muir, Bart., of Blairdrummond
Brig.-Gen. J. H. Campbell, Inverardoch, Doune

Rev. Thomas Crawford, B.D., Orchill, Braco
Brig.-Gen. Arch. Stirling of Keir
George Crabbie of Blairhoyle
James M'Anish, Doune
John G. Stewart, Aultwharrie, Dunblane

County Clerks and Treasurers--David Marshall and T. B. Marshall, County Buildings, Perth, who is Clerk of Standing Joint-Committee, and other Council Committees, except where ·otherwise noted.

County Medical Officer and Chief Medical Officer for Districts —Dr. John T. Graham, County Buildings, Perth.

County Sanitary Inspector and Chief Sanitary Inspector for Districts—Robert M'Nicoll, County Buildings, Perth.

County Tuberculosis Officer—Dr. David Dempster, County Buildings, Perth.

The Statutory Meetings of the Council are fixed for second Monday of May second Monday of October, and third Monday of December.

LIST OF REPRESENTATIVES FROM PARISH COUNCILS TO DISTRICT COMMITTEES OF PERTH COUNTY.

I.—PERTH DISTRICT.

The County Councillors within the District as above, also the Representatives of the Parish Councils as follows:—

	Name.	Address.	Parish.
1	Robert P. M'Lagan,	East Mid Lamberkin	Aberdalgie
2	William S. Baillie	Drumhead, Abernethy	Abernethy
3	Fred. S. Molison	Lochton, Inchture	Abernyte
4	George W. Murray	Lochelbank, Glenfarg	Arngask
5	Duncan Robertson	Rashielea, by Stanley	Auchtergaven
6	Geo. Pitcaithly	West Dron, Bridge of Earn	Dron
7	Alex. B. Stevens	Mains of Kilgraston	Dunbarney
8	William Niven	Farmer, Loan, Errol	Errol
9	R. W. G. Cameron	Drumharvie, Gask, Auchter-arder	Findo-Gask
10	Rev. J. Paterson Brownlie	The Manse	Forgandenny
11	Wm. Nairn	Forteviot Farm	Forteviot
12	A. J. Macdonald	Castlehill	Inchture
13	John W. Lawson	Goddens, Errol	Kilspindie
14	Major W. F. Middleton	of Baldarroch, Murthly	Kinclaven
15	Rev. R. S. Davidson	Kinfauns Manse	Kinfauns
16	Rev. J. M. Anderson	The Manse, Kinnaird	Kinnaird
17	Col. Drummond Hay	Seggieden, Kinfauns	Kinnoull
18	John Prain	Inglewood, Invergowrie	Longforgan
19	Thos. W. Reid,	The Haugh, Methven	Methven
20	William Baxter	Tophead, Stanley	Moneydie
21	William Robertson	St. Paul's Square, Perth	Perth
22	William Graham	Netherby, Stanley	Redgorton
23	J. Moncrieff Wright	of Kinmonth	Rhynd
24	Jas. G. Bryden	Newmains, Scone	Scone
25	Hon, A. D. Murray	Pitfour Castle, Glencarse	St. Madoes
26	David Morton	North Muirton, Perth	Tibbermore

Chairman—Colonel Smythe.

District Clerk and Treasurer—D. Macnab, solicitor, Perth.
County Collector for District—D. Macnab, solicitor, Perth.
District Surveyor—Alex. Macarthur, Feus Road, Perth

II.—BLAIRGOWRIE OR EASTERN DISTRICT.

The County Councillors within the District as above, also the Representatives of the Parish Council, as follows:—

	Name.	Address.	Parish.
1	Jas. F. Murray	Ellengrove, Meigle	Alyth
2	Rev. A. W. Smith, B.D.	The Manse, Bendochy	Bendochy
3	Robert Clark	Beecroft, Blairgowrie.	Blairgowrie
4	A. E. Cox	of Dungarthill, Dunkeld	Caputh
5	Robert Morris	St. Matthews, Woodside	Cargill
6	George M'Ritchie	Reichip	Clunie
7	Hugh Martin	Flowerdale, Kinrossie, Perth	Collace
8	Thomas Ferguson	Princeland, Coupar-Angus	Coupar-Angus
9	Sydney G. Meacher	Marlee House, Blairgowrie	Kinloch
10	John Stewart	Mains of Dounie, Kirkmichael	Kirkmichael
11	Alex. Smith	Cranley, Meikleour	Lethendy
12	Sir George Kinloch	of Kinloch, Bart., Muirton, by Blairgowrie	Meigle
13	Alex. Crichton	South Littleton, Rattray	Rattray
14	Peter Peebles	Townhead Farm, Balbeggie	St. Martins

Chairman—William Henderson, Esq.

District Clerk and Treasurer—J. B. Miller, solicitor, Blairgowrie. County Collector for District—J. B. Miller, solicitor, Blairgowrie. District Surveyor—George Wyllie, Blairgowrie.

III.—HIGHLAND DISTRICT.

The County Councillors within the District as above, also the Representatives of the Parish Councils, as follows:—

	Name.	Address.	Parish.
1	D. D. Macdonald	Atholl Arms Hotel, Blair-Atholl	Blair-Atholl
2	John Menzies	Innkeeper, Coshieville, Aberfeldy	Dull
3	Alex. Campbell	Easter Tullymully, Dunkeld	Dunkeld and Dowally
4	Arch. Cameron	Merchant, Kinloch-Rannoch	Fortingall
5	P. Macnaughton	Farmer, Remony	Kenmore
6	Wm. Alex. Rae	Douglasfield, Murthly	Little Dunkeld
7	Capt. J. M. S. Steuart	Tullypowrie House, Strathtay	Logierait
8	Capt John Marshall	Corlissan, Killiecrankie	Moulin
9	Rev. Angus Boyd	Manse, Weem, Aberfeldy	Weem

Chairman—Major J. Stewart Robertson.

District Clerks and Treasurers—Hugh Mitchell and Buckham W. Liddell, W.S., solicitors, Pitlochry. County Collector for District—Hugh Mitchell. District Surveyor—James S. Cree, Aberfeldy.

IV.—CENTRAL DISTRICT.

The County Councillors within the District as above ; also
the Representatives of the Parish Councils, as follows :—

	Name.	Address.	Parish.
1	Robert Wilson	Farmer, Mid Strathie	Auchterarder
2	Major Findlay	Machany House	Blackford
3	C. D. M. Ross	Solicitor, Crieff	Crieff
4	John Carmichael	Joiner, Dundas Street, Comrie	Comrie
5	Robert Matthew	Estate Overseer, Duncrub	Dunning
6	Captain W. A. H. Drummond Moray	of Abercairney, Crieff,	Fowlis-Wester
7	W. Guild	Farmer, Glenquay, Glendevon. Dollar.	Glendevon
8	Archd. J. P. Murray	Logie House, Methven	Logiealmond
9	John Anderson	Parkside, Madderty	Madderty
10	William Finlayson	Carse of Strowan, Crieff	Monzievaird and Strowan
11	W. Forbes M'Laren	Balruddrie, Rumbl'g Bridge	Muckhart
12	Rev. A Cross, M.A.	The Manse, Muthill	Muthill
13	Daniel M'Intosh	East Mains, Colquhalzie, Machany	Trinity-Gask

Chairman—The Earl of Mansfield.
District Clerk and Treasurer—Malcolm Finlayson, solicitor
Crieff. County Collector for District—M. Finlayson. District
Surveyor—Alexander Roberton, Crieff.

V.—WESTERN DISTRICT.

The County Councillors within the District as above,
the Representatives of the Parish Councils, as follows :—

	Name.	Address.	Parish.
1	R. H. Beckett	Dundhu, Aberfoyle	Aberfoyle
2	John Barnett	Farmer, Garrick, Braco	Ardoch
3	John M'Dougall	Clan Alpine Cott., Strathyre	Balquhidder
4	William Cairns	Glenfinlas, Brig-o'-Turk	Callander
5	Col. A. W. Hay Drummond	of Cromlix, Dunblane	Dunblane and Lecropt
6	John Scrimgeour	Doune Lodge, Doune	Kilmadock
7	Peter Walker	Clachaig House, Killin	Killin
8	Andrew M'Farlane	Dripend, by Stirling	Kincardine
9	T. N. Johnston	Malling, Port of Monteith	Port of Monteith

Chairman—Brig-Gen. Stirling.
District Clerk and Treasurer—John Stewart, solicitor,
Dunblane. County Collector for District—John Stewart.
District Surveyor—W. L. Gibson, C.E., Dunblane.

MEMBERS OF DISTRICT LICENSING COURTS AND APPEAL COURTS.

I.—DISTRICT LICENSING COURTS.

Justice of Peace Members.	County Council Members.

PERTH DISTRICT.

J. Moncrieff Wright	John F. Smith
Sir Robert D. Moncreiffe, Bart.	James Fenwick
Colonel Drummond Hay	Geo. Pople
Robert Keay	David Hardie

BLAIRGOWRIE OR EASTERN DISTRICT.

T. J. Gardiner	George Tasker
Wm. Whitson	J. M. Hodge
James Chalmers	Wm. Henderson
Hugh Martin	Col. Clerk Rattray

HIGHLAND DISTRICT.

Robert Inglis	A. Macdonald
James Scott	Colonel Steuart Fothringham
Provost Haggart	D. Stewart Fergusson
Hugh Mitchell	Major A. Blair Stewart

CENTRAL DISTRICT.

William Brown	J. P. Mitchell
David Keith Murray	A. Gregor Dixon
John M'Nee	William Gardiner
Capt. O. H. Graham Stirling	Wm. Cairns

WESTERN DISTRICT.

Charles Murray Stewart	Donald M'Laren
A. H. Anderson	J. G. Stewart
Wm. Brydie	W. Watson Murray
James Rodger	James M'Anish

II.—COUNTY APPEAL COURT.

Col. A. M. B. Grahame	Thomas Hollingworth
William Morison	Alexander MacDuff
John M. Matthew	W. O. Macpherson
Stuart Honeyman	R. R. Constable
Wm. Henderson	J. Stewart Robertson
Norman J. Nasmyth	G. T. Ewing
Geo. Bell	Brig.-Gen. Archibald Stirling

III.—BURGH OF PERTH APPEAL COURT.

Justices of the Peace.	Magistrates.
D. Macnab	The Lord Provost
Hon. Alex. D. Murray	The Four Bailies and
F. Norie-Miller	The Dean of Guild of Perth
Wm. Morison	
Jas. Barlas	
J. Simpson	

COUNTY ROAD BOARD.

N. J. Nasmyth, Aberargie
John F. Smith. Bridge of Earn
Col. Smythe, Methven
C. A. Murray, Stanley
Charles Hutchison, Scone
Alex. Macduff, Kinnoull
David Hardie, Errol
Thos. Hollingworth, Inchture
William Henderson, Cargill
A. M. Ferguson, Alyth
J. M. Hodge, Glenericht
W. H. Cox, Caputh
Chas. Boyd, Coupar-Angus
Col. Clerk Rattray, Rattray
Colonel Steuart Fothering-
ham, Little Dunkeld
J. Stewart Robertson, Dulland
Weem
A. M'Donald, Fortingall

Wm. Fenton, Pitlochry
Major Blair Stewart, Moulin
Major C. H. Graham Stirling,
Monzievaird & Crieff
The Earl of Mansfield, Logie-
almond
G. T. Ewing, Pitkellony,
Muthill
Wm. Gardiner, Trinity-Gask
Lord Rollo, Dunning
Andrew Thomson, Glendevon
Donald M'Laren, Callander
and Balquidder
Brig.-Gen. Stirling. Dunblane
and Lecropt
Rev. Tho . Crawford, Ardoch
Brig Cen. J. H. Campbell, Kil-
madock

Chairman—The Earl of Mansfield.   Quorum 5.

COUNTY FINANCE COMMITTEE.

The Earl of Moray, St. Madoes
James M. Hodge, Glenericht
W. H. Cox, Caputh
Donald M'Laren, Callander
and Balquhidder
John F. Smith, Bridge of Earn
Lord Forteviot, Dupplin
Alex. Macduff (Kinnoull)
William Henderson (Cargill)
J. M. Matthew (St. Martins)
J. Stewart Robertson (Dull
and Weem)
Colonel Steuart Fothring-
ham (Little Dunkeld)

The Marquis of Breadalbane
(Kenmore)
The Duke of Atholl, K.T.
C.B., M.V O., D.S.O. (Blair
Atholl)
The Earl of Mansfield (Logie-
almond)
Geo. T. Ewing (Muthill)
W. Gardiner (Trinity Gask)
James P. Kennaway (Auchter-
arder)
Brig.-Gen. Arch. Stirling,
Dunblane and Lecropt
J. G. Stewart (Dunblane)
Col. Smythe (Methven)

The Earl of Mansfield, Chairman.   Five a Quorum.

STANDING JOINT COMMITTEE.

Appointed by County Council
1. Col. Smythe, (Methven.)
2. Wm. Henderson (Cargill)
3. W. C. Macpherson (Blairgowrie) (N)
4. The Duke of Atholl (Dunk.)
5. The Earl of Mansfield,
(Logiealmond)
6. A. Gregor Dixon (Fowlis
Wester)
7. John Graham Stewart
(Dunblane)

*Appointed by Commissioner
of Supply.*
1. Lord Kinnaird
2. N. J. Nasmyth
3. Brig.-Gen. Stirling]
4. A. G. Maxtone Graham
5. Col. Drummond Hay
6. Alex. Macduff .
7. Col Steuart Fothringham

Ex-officio—The Sheriff of the County.
Chairman—Colonel Smythe. *Quorum*
Chief Constable—Matthew J. Martin.

B

COMMITTEE OF COUNTY ON BILLS.

The Earl of Mansfield, Chairman.

The Earl of Mansfield (Logie-almond)
Sir J. H. Ramsay (Alyth)
J. Stewart Robertson (Dull and Weem)
Colonel Steuart Fothringham Little Dunkeld)
David Hardie (Errol)
Charles Hutchison (Scone)

Wm. Fenton (Pitlochry)
W. Cairns (Blackford)
Andrew Thomson(Glendevon)
W. Watson Murray (Aberfoyle)
Brig.-Gen. Stirling (Dunblane and Lecropt)
John Graham Stewart (Dunblane)
Wm. Henderson (Cargill)

Three a Quorum.

COMMITTEE UNDER COMMISSIONERS OF SUPPLY ACTS FOR DISPOSING OF CLAIMS TO BE ENROLLED.

Acts 19 and 20 cap. 93 and 20 Victoria cap. 11.

The Duke of Atholl
Col. Smythe
A. G. Maxtone Graham,Esq.
Lieut.-Col. Stirling of Kier
Sir R. D. Moncreiffe, Bart.

Alex. Macduff,Esq.,of Bonhard
James Speid, Esq.
Sheriff Sym
A. H. Anderson, Esq.

Col. Smythe, Chairman.
Three a Quorum.

DISTRICT BOARD OF CONTROL.

I.—APPOINTED BY COUNTY COUNCIL.

Chas. Hutchison, Scone
Alex. Macduff, Kinnoull
The Earl of Moray, St. Madoes
John M. Matthew, St. Martins
W. H. Cox, Caputh
Chas. Boyd, Coupar-Angus

Colonel Steuart Fothringham, Little Dunkeld
D. S. Fergusson, Logierait
Andrew Thomson, Glendevon
W. A. Dron, Crieff (East)
James M'Anish, Doune

II.—APPOINTED BY TOWN COUNCIL OF PERTH.

Lord-Provost Wotherspoon ; Alex. Frazer, Dean of Guild

III.—APPOINTED TO REPRESENT PARISH COUNCILS.

David Ferrier, Edin Terrace, Perth.
George Pople, Newhouse. Perth.
Wm. Whitson, Isla Park, Coupar-Angus.
Robert Inglis, Old Blair, Blair-Atholl.
Wm. Brown, Kirkton, Trinity-Gask.
Lieut.-Colonel A. W. Hay-Drummond, of Cromlix, Dunblane.

IV.— CO-OPTED MEMBER.

Mrs. Grierson, Laguna, Murthly.
Chairman, Col. Steuart Fothringham.
Vice-Chairman, W. H. Cox, Esq.
Three a Quorum.

Medical Superintendent, Dr. Lewis C. Bruce, Perth District Asylum, Murthly.

Joint Clerks and Treasurers } David Marshall, T. B. Marshall { County Buildings, Perth

DISEASES OF (ANIMALS) ACTS, 1894 AND 1896.

Local Authority—The County Council.

EXECUTIVE COMMITTEE UNDER SAID ACTS.

I.—County Councillors.

1. Geo. Pople, Tibbermore
2. John F. Smith, Bridge of Earn
3. Lord Forteviot, Forteviot
4. David Hardie (Errol)
5. Thomas Hollingworth, Inchture
6. Jas. Fenwick, Redgorton
7. John M. Matthew, St Martins
8. Wm Henderson, Cargill
9. George Tasker, Meigle
10. R. R. Constable, Kirkmichael
11. R. Inglis, Dunkeld
12. D. Stewart Fergusson, Logierait
13. A. Macdonald, Fortingall
14. Major C. H. Graham Stirling, Monzievaird and Crieff
15. Wm. Gardiner, Trinity Gask
16. Campbell Willison, Killin
17. Donald M'Laren, Callander and Balquidder
18. W. Watson Murray, Aberfoyle and Monteith

II.—Rated Occupiers and otherwise qualified.

1. Thomas Ferguson, Princeland, Coupar Angus.
2. W. J. Grant, Dengarth, Blairgowrie
3. William Brydie, Shielhill Braco.

Chairman—Wm. Henderson, Esq.

Quorum 3.

Clerks—David Marshall and T. B. Marshall, County Buildings, Perth.

Inspectors.

Perth	District,	J. G. Reynard, V.S., Perth
East Carse	do	W. Ferguson, V.S., Dundee
West Carse	do	John Brown, V.S., 51 York Place, Perth.
Arngask	do	John Hepburn, V.S., Milnathort
Auchterarder	do	W. Donaldson, V.S., Auchterarder
Crieff	do	Wm. Watt, V.S., Crieff
Western	do	D. Macfarlane, V.S., Doune
Coupar-Angus	do	W. S. Clark, V.S., Coupar-Angus
Alyth	do	Murray Lornie, V.S., Alyth
Blairgowrie	do	William Nairn, V.S., Blairgowrie
Highland	do	John Panton, V.S., Blair-Atholl and Killin
Ardoch	do	Donald Wooley, V.S., Braco

COMMITTEE OF MANAGEMENT OF COUNTY HALL, &o.

Col. Smythe of Methven.
Arch. Murray, Esq.
The Duke of Atholl, M.V.O., D SO, C.B.
Lord Forteviot.
J. Stewart Robertson, Esq.
The Earl of Mansfield
Lieut.-Col. Arch, Stirling.
Atholl Macgregor, Esq.
Col. Steuart Fothringham.
Col. P. R. Burn Clerk Rattray of Craighall, Blairgowrie
William Keith Murray, Yr. of Ochtertyre, Crieff

David Marshall, Clerk.

COUNTY VALUATION COMMITTEE OF PERTHSHIRE

(APPOINTED UNDER ACT 42, 44, AND 45 VICT., CAP. 42)

Three a Quorum.

James Fenwick (Redgorton)
Colonel Smythe, Methven
Thos. Hollingworth (Inchture)
Vacant
Sir J. H. Ramsay (Alyth)
James M. Hodge (Glenericht)
A. M. Ferguson (Alyth)
Chas. Boyd, Coupar-Angus
Colonel Steuart Fothringham (Little Dunkeld)
J. Stewart Robertson (Dull and Weem)
David Hardie (Errol)

Capt. F. de Sales La Terriere (Rannoch)
A. Clow (Aberfeldy)
A. Gregor Dixon (Fowlis Wester)
James P. Kennaway (Auchterarder)
W. Gardiner (Trinity-Gask)
W. A. Dron, Crieff (East)
Campbell Willison (Killin)
Donald M'Laren (Callander & Balquhidder)
W. Watson Murray (Aberfoyle

Chairman—Colonel Smythe.

Assessor—Chas. Craig, 42 Tay Street, Perth

WEIGHTS AND MEASURES.

William Scott, Inspector for the County of Perth.
Office—County Buildings, Perth.

PERTHSHIRE CONSTABULARY.

Standing Joint Committee.

APPOINTED BY COUNTY COUNCIL.

Wm. Henderson, Cargill
W. C. Macpherson, Blairgowrie
Earl of Mansfield, Logiealmond
J. G. Stewart, Dunblane

The Duke of Atholl
Colonel Smythe, Methven
A. Gregor Dixon (Fowlis Wester)

APPOINTED BY COMMISSIONERS OF SUPPLY.

Lord Kinnaird
Brig.-Gen. Arch. Stirling of Keir
A. G. Maxtone Graham

Alex. Macduff
Colonel Drummond Hay.
Colonel Steuart Fothringham
N. J. Nasmyth

Ex-Officio, Sheriff of Perthshire. Six a Quorum

Chairman—Colonel Smythe

Chief Constable—Matthew J. Martin

Depute Chief Constable—D. Macpherson

Superintendents—D. Macpherson, Perth, and James Kidd, Dunblane; Inspectors—John Robertson, Perth; A. Mitchell, Blairgowrie; John Macpherson, Crieff; and D. Stuart, Pitlochry.

Detective Sergeants—D. Moir and A. Davidson, Perth.

Sergeants—A. Gatherum, Aberfeldy; D. Allan, Callander; R. Bruce, Killin; A' Cameron, Pittochry; A. Wilson, Alyth; H. Rae, Inchture; Alexander Malcolm, Auchterarder; and John Grant, Dunblane.

Stations of the Men.

a Aberfoyle
a c Aberfeldy
a Abernethy
Almondbank
a c Alyth
a c Auchterarder
Balbeggie
Ballinluig
a Blackford
a Birnam
a Bridge of Earn
Blair-Atholl
abc Blairgowrie
Bankfoot
Braco
Burrelton
a Comrie
a c Callander

a Crianlarich
abc Crieff
a Coupar-Angus
Dunkeld
abc Dunblane
a Doune
a Dunning
a Errol
Forgandenny
Fortingall
Fowlis Wester
Gartmore
Glencarse
Glenfarg
Glenshee
Grandtully
a c Inchture
Invergowrie
Kenmore

a c Killin
Kinloch-Rann'ch
Kirkmichael
Lochearnhead
Logiealmond
Longforgan
a Meigle
a Methven
a Muckhart
a Muthill
a New Rattray
New Scone
a b Perth
abc Pitlochry
a Stanley
Spittalfield
St. Fillans
Thornhill

A Station House with Police Cells, at places marked thus (a)

The Superintendents and Inspectors are stationed at the places marked thus (b)

The Sergeants are stationed at the places marked thus (c)

GENERAL PRISON FOR SCOTLAND.

Dr Skene, medical officer and superintendent of Criminal Lunatic Department; Rev. Jas. M'Kenzie, chaplain; Very Rev. Canon Welsh, visiting R.C. priest; Very Rev. Canon Farquhar, visiting Episcopalian clergyman; Mr J. M'Graw, store warder.

This prison is under the direction of four Commissioners, appointed under the Prisons (Scotland) Act (1877), who have also a superintendence of all prisons in Scotland. The expense of the establishment is defrayed from the public funds.

LIST OF MEMBERS OF THE INSURANCE COMMITTEE FOR THE COUNTY OF PERTH.

PERSONS APPOINTED BY THE COUNTY COUNCIL:—

John F. Smith, Eastfield, Bridge of Earn

Geo. Pople, Newhouse, Perth

J. M. Hodge, Solicitor, Blairgowrie

Provost Chalmers, Coupar-Angus

Wm. Fenton, cabinetmaker, Pitlochry

David D. Macdonald, Atholl Arms Hotel, Blair Atholl

George T. Ewing, Pitkellony, Muthill

Provost Mungall, Crieff

Rev. Thos. Crawford, B.D., of Orchill, Braco

Ex-Bailie Hume, Dunblane

Mrs. Shearer, Ashgrove, Dunblane

Miss M. A. Pagan, Dallerie, Crieff

Dr. John Mackay, Dallavon, Aberfeldy

Dr. John Liddell, Errol

PERSONS APPOINTED BY THE SCOTTISH INSURANCE COMMISSIONERS—

Lady Chapman, King James Place, Perth

Mrs. Geo. Keith Murray, The Cottage, Abercairney

Miss Blackett, Inverard, Aberfoyle

R. Speedie, Druggist, Crieff

Thos. Thomson, jun., Westfield, Rattray, Blairgowrie

Provost MacDonald, Callander

Dr. A. C. Buist, Woodend, Dunblane

Dr. W. A. Taylor, Riversdale, Perth

PERSONS APPOINTED TO REPRESENT INSURED PERSONS—
By "A" Societies.

A. C. Campbell, solicitor, Perth

Miss Jean Maxtone, Strathallan, Machany

John Stewart, solicitor, Dunblane

James London, Longforgan, by Dundee

William Baxter, farmer, Tophead, Stanley

John A. Gardiner, Balmuick, Comrie

J. M. Stalker, The Lodge, Huntingtower

James Swan, Garryside, Blair-Atholl

J. M. Clark, Balmoral Road, Rattray, Blairgowrie Perth

J. A. Miller, Fairies Road, Perth

Robert C. Marshall, Ardchoile, Pitlochry

Wm. Brunton Thornton, Burrell Square, Crieff

D. Watson, Pitheavlis Bank, Perth

R. C. Haxton, Queen's Road, Scone, Perth

William Pickard, 2 Addison Terrace, Crieff

Edward R. Wright, Rowan Cottage, Ruthven Street, Auchterarder

James A. M'Gregor, Birchbank, Muirton Place, Perth

George Stewart, Springwells, Dunkeld

J. Methven, 1 Hawarden Terrace, Perth

Mrs. John A. Stewart, Brafassi, Barnhill, Perth

Robert R. Bruce, 2 Spens Crescent, Perth

Lady Haldane, Foswell, Auchterarder

Ex-Provost John Smith, High Street, Blairgowrie

James Rodger, Keir Estates Office, Dunblane

David Haggart, 209 High St., Perth

John M'Intosh, Rose Cresc'nt, Glasgow Road, Perth

PERSONS APPOINTED TO REPRESENT INSURED. PERSONS—*Cont.*

By " B " Societies.

John Scrimgeour, Sydney Villa, Crieff

Miss Macdonald, Newlands, Scone

Vacancy

Alex. Russell, 4 St. Catherine's Road, Perth

James Thomson, 9 Shield's Place, Perth

Wm. Paterson, Murrryshall Road, Scone

John Stewart, 33 Scott Street, Perth

Thomas Duncan, Knockearn, Needless Road, Perth

TO REPRESENT DEPOSIT CONTRIBUTORS—

The Hon. Mrs. Stirling, Keir, Dunblane.

APPOINTED BY MEDICAL PRACTITIONERS—

Dr. Henderson, Ardmhor, Scone.

Dr. Burgess, Stanley.

Chairman—J. M. Hodge, Esq., Solicitor, Blairgowrie.

Vice-Chairman—Wm. Pickard, Esq., Crieff.

Clerk—T. B. Marshall, County Buildings, Perth.

BURGH OF PERTH INSURANCE COMMITTEE.

LIST OF MEMBERS.

Ex-Lord Provost Macnab, *Chairman.*

Robert Callan, *Vice-Chairman*

Mrs. Martin

Miss Macnab

Mrs. Ritchie

Mrs. Smith

Miss Smith

Miss Grant

Dr. Bisset

Councillor Bowie

James Brown

Peter Bruce

Ex-Bailie Calderwood

John Clark

Alexander Duff

Robert Davidson

John Drummond

David Edwards

·Councillor Fisher

Thomas Harley

J. Lennox Hobson

R. Hamilton

Dr. John Hume

Dr. Menzies

Alexander Murray

George M'Leod

John Nairn

William Pearson

Councillor Rae

Duncan Robertson

A. L. Rumgay

Hugh Sinclair

Councillor Simpson

Andrew Smith

Andrew Staig

John B. Stuart

Councillor Taylor

William Taylor

Dr. Trotter

Lord Provost Wotherspoon

Clerk, William C. Burt, Solicitor, 36 High Street, Perth.

COMMISSIONERS OF SUPPLY FOR PERTHSHIRE.

Convener—Colonel Smythe of Methven.

A. H. Anderson, factor for, Kippendavie

The Duke of Atholl, K.T., C.B., M.V.O., D.S.O., Blair Castle, Blair-Atholl

Francis Balfour of Kindrogan

Chas. Boyd, solicitor, Coupar-Angus, as factor for Miss Murray of Lintrose.

The Marquis of Breadalbane, Taymouth Castle, Aberfeldy

Col. Campbell of Achalader, Blairgowrie

Brig.-Gen. Campbell of Inverardoch, Doune

James Charles Calder of Roughfoldslap, etc.

John Jos. Calder of Ardargie

W. Leslie Christie, of Lochdochart, Killin

A. E. Cox of Dungarthill, by Dunkeld

W. H. Cox of Snaigow and Clunie

W. Bruce Dickie of Whitehills

Captain Drummond of Megginch

Charles C. Duncan of Easter Denhead, Coupar Angus

Lord Elibank, Peebles

Henry D. Erskine of Cardross, Stirling

Lieut. J. F. Erskine, yr. of Cardross, Stirling

George T. Ewing, Pitkellony, factor for the Earl of Ancaster

Geo. Fleming of Netherton of Claywhat, Blairgowrie

Lord Forteviot, Dupplin Castle

Colonel Steuart Fothringham of Grandtully, Murthly

J. M. Fraser of Invermay

Thomas Johnson Gilbert of Coldoch

The Marquis of Graham, Buchanan Castle

A. G. Maxtone Graham of Cultoquhey

Alastair Erskine Graham, 19 Inverleith Row, Edinburgh

James Patrick Grant of Kilgraston

J. G. Hay Halkett of Ballendoch, Meigle

Col. J. A. G. Drummond Hay of Seggieden

Robt. Inglis, Old Blair, Blair-Atholl, factor for the Duke of Atholl

Sir Robert Jardine, Bart., of Lanrick Doune

C. Y. Kinloch of Gourdie, Meikleour

Lord Kinnaird, Rossie Priory

R. J. Landale of Pitmedden, Edinburgh

David C. R. Lindsay of Ashintully and Glendevon

J. Laing Low of Butterstone

The Earl of Mansfield, Scone Palace

Wm. H. Marshall of Callander
J. A. Menzies of Pitnacree, Ballinluig
Major William Lindsay Mercer of Huntingtower
Major Middleton, Baldarroch, Murthly
Sir Robert D. Moncreiffe, Bart., of Moncreiffe
D. Scott Moncrieff, W.S., of Easter Downhill, Edinburgh
The Duke of Montrose
J J. Mowbray of Balrudderie, Dollar
W. H. Mungall, Croftweit, Crieff
Sir Patrick K. Murray of Ochtertyre, Crieff
D. Keith Murray, Ochtertyre, as factor for Sir Patrick K. Murray
Wm. Keith Murray of Fowlis-Wester
William Watson Murray, as factor for the Duke of Montrose
F. F. M'Donald, solicitor, Arbroath, as factor for trustees of the late Adam Fraser
R. M'Gillewie, banker, Dunkeld, as factor for Balnakeilly
Alex. Macduff of Bonhard
W. C. Macpherson of Blairgowrie
John M'Nee, Crieff
Norman J. Nasmyth, of Glenfarg, Abernethy.
George Pople, Newhouse
Sir Jas. H. Ramsay of Bamff, Bart., Alyth
Professor Ramsay of Drumore

Ernest F. Robertson of Auchleeks
J. Stewart-Robertson of Edradynate .
James Rodger, Keir Mains, Dunblane, factor for Brig.-Gen. Archibald Stirling of Keir
Lord Rollo and Dunning, Duncrub Park, Dunning
Dr. P. W. Shaw of Westerton and Blacklunans, Blairgowrie
Rev H. A. Graham Sheppard of Rednoch, Stirling
Col. Smythe of Methven
James Speid of Forneth
Robt. T. N. Speir of Culdees, Muthill
Julian M'Carty Steele of Evelick
A. B. Stewart of Balnakeilly
John Malcolm Steuart Steuart of Ballechin
Brig.-Gen. A. Stirling of Keir, Dunblane
Capt. C. H. Graham Stirling of Strowan
John Sutherland, Inverness, factor for Highland Railway Company
William Neish Walker of Balgersho
Harry Giles Walker, yr. of Balgersho
J. M. White of Pilmores, Dundee
Thomas Ernest Lyndoch Hill Whitson of Parkhill
William Whitson of Isla Park
J. Moncrieff Wright, of Kinmonth, Bridge of Earn
Sir James R. Witson, Bart., of Invertrossachs, Callander

MEMBERS OF THE EDUCATION AUTHORITY OF THE COUNTY OF PERTH.

Elected 11th April, 1919.

7 Higher Grade Schools, 4 of which are Junior Student Centres. 161 Primary Schools. No. of children on Rolls, 17,964.

First Electoral Division—William A. Barclay, Esq., Savings Bank, Perth; James G. Bryden, Esq., New Mains, Scone; Sir Samuel Chapman, King's Place, Perth; John Dow, Esq., Burnbank Terrace, Perth; Frank Eastman, Esq., of Messrs. Pullar & Sons, Perth; George F. Farquhar, Esq., 16 Inchhead Terrace, Perth; Francis Norie-Miller, Esq., Cleeve, Perth; Dr. Robert Stirling, Atholl Place, Perth; John Ritchie, Esq., Rockbank, Perth.

Second Electoral Division—Alexander Campbell, Esq., Daisy Cottage, Stanley; Lord Forteviot, Dupplin Castle, Perth; Alexander Graham, Esq., The Hill, Errol; Rev. R. G. Macdonald, Pitcairngreen, Almondbank; James Paton, Esq., Obney, Bankfoot.

Third Electoral Division—Col. Clerk-Rattray of Craighall, Blairgowrie; Sir George Kinloch, Bart., of Kinloch, Meigle; Robert Morris, Esq., St. Matthew's, Woodside, Coupar-Angus; Rev. Charles Stewart, The Manse, Coupar-Angus; Rev. Robert Stewart, St. Mary's Manse, Blairgowrie.

Fourth Electoral Division—The Duchess of Atholl, Blair Castle, Blair-Atholl; Dr. George F. Barbour, Bonskeid, Pitlochry; Alexander Campbell, Esq., Boreland, Fearnan, Aberfeldy; Rev. John M'Ainsh, U.F. Manse, Strathbraan, Dunkeld; James Macnaughton, Esq., Edragoll, Aberfeldy.

Fifth Flectoral Division—Miss Haldane. Cloan, Auchterarder; S. Graham Mickel, Esq., solicitor, Crieff; Peter M'Intyre, Esq., Tighnablair, Comrie; Lord Rollo, of Duncrub, Dunning; James M. Taylor, Esq., manufacturer, Blackford.

Sixth Electoral Division—Alexander H. Anderson, Esq., The Firs, Dunblane; James M'Anish, Esq., Balkerach Street, Doune; Thomas Macdonald. Esq., Ach-na-Coile, Callander; Donald M'Laren, Esq., Bracklinn, Callander; James D. M'Rae, Esq., Tigh-n-fhinn, Killin.

Offices of the Authority—Rose Terrace, Perth.
Chairman, F. Norie-Miller, Esq.
Vice-Chairman, Thomas Macdonald, Esq.
Executive Officer, R. Martin Bates.
Director of Education, John M. Dawson, M.A.
Principal Medical Officer—
D. J. M'Leish, M.A.; B.Sc. M.D.; D.P.H.
Architect and Master of Works, A. Watt Allison.

PERTH ACADEMY AND SHARP'S INSTITUTION SCHOOL STAFF.

Rector—Edward Smart, B.A., B.Sc. (Lond.), F.R S.E.
Lady Superintendent—Miss Katherine C. Caird, M.A. (St. And.)

HIGHER DEPARTMENT.

English --William M. Kerr, M.A. (Glasg.), Senior Master ; David
Coutts, M.A. (Aber.) ; Miss M. E. Kerr, M.A. (Edin.) ; Miss
M. H. Robertson, M.A. (Aber.); Miss M. F. Kerr. M.A.
(Glas.); Miss M. Robertson, M.A. (Edin.).

Classics -William Gow, M.A. (Glasg.), B.A. (Oxon.), Senior
Master; Miss Blanche L. Watt, M.A. (Edin); Miss Grace
M. Scott, M.A. (St. And.); James Murray, M.A. (Aber.); Miss
M. A. Mackinnon, M.A. (Edin).

Modern Languages --Jean J. Buhrer, Cert. d'et Sup., Senior
Master; Miss Susan F. Mitchell, M.A. (Glasg.); Miss
Florence I. W. Littlejohn, M.A. (St. And.)

Mathematics and Arithmetic—John Watt, M.A. (Aber), Senior
Master; Miss Jessie Murray, M.A. (Aber.); Sinclair Grant,
M.A. (Glasg.); Miss Margaret H. Robertson, M.A. (Aber.);
Miss Maggie M'Keand, M.A. (Leeds); Wm. P. M'Pherson,
B.Sc. (Glas.) ; Miss M. A. Mackinnon M.A. (Edin.).

Science--Edward J. Balfour, M.A , B.Sc. (St. And.). Senior
Master; William G. Mitchell, Second Master; Sinclair
Grant, M A. (Glasg.); Wm. P. Macpherson, B.Sc. (Glasg.);
Miss Mary H. Tolmie, M.A. (Edin.); Mrs. Mary Ann Atkin
(Interim).

Commercial Subjects--James Murray. M.A. (Aber.). ; Miss Alice
Garden, F.C.T.S. ; Miss Jeanie M. Hossack.

Drawing, Painting. and Design--D. Scott Murray, Art Master,
Senior Master; James Smieton, Art Master (Leipzig Dip-
loma), Second Master; Miss Elspeth S. Galloway. Art
Diploma, E.S.A

Workshop and Manual Instruction--John Mitchell, Cert. City
and Guilds, London; Leipzig Diploma, and Medal for
Metal-Work and Modelling.

Needlework and Domestic Subjects--Miss M. G. Deas, First-
Class Diploma in Cookery, Housewifery, Laundry, from
Atholl Crescent, Edinburgh ; and Miss Jessie MacKinnon.

LOWER DEPARTMENT.

John Asher, F.S.A. (Scot.), Head Master; Miss Mary B. Richardson, Infant Mistress; Miss Lizzie Gordon, Miss Isabella Howie; Miss Mary J. P. Barrie, M.A. (St. And.); Miss Annie B. Macfarlane; Miss Linda Carmichael; Miss Annie B. M'Kim; Miss Stewartina J. Miller; Miss Catherine M. Nish.

SPECIAL SUBJECTS.

Music—Pianoforte- Miss Jane R. Cormack, Senior Mistress; Miss Nellie G. Smart, A.R.C.M.; Miss Helen E. Kinnoch, A.R.C.M. *Singing—*Stephen Richardson, and F. Midgley, F.R.C.O.

*Swedish Gymnastics and Dancing—*Miss Græme Leslie, Diploma, Dunfermline College of Hygiene and Physical Education.

*Boys Rifle Club—*David Smith, Instructor.

*Janitors—*David Smith, John C. Chaplin, James Chamberlain, Charles B. Morris.

PUBLIC ELEMENTARY SCHOOLS IN CITY OF PERTH.

Caledonian Road Sch....Hugh Leslie, Miss Stewart, and assists.
Central District do. ...W. Paterson, Miss J. Kaye, and assts.
Kinnoull   do. ...David Murray, Miss Smith   „
Northern District do. ...Dougald Walker, Miss Brough, „
Southern District do. ...Wm. P. Nairne, Miss M'Lagan, „
Western   do. ...John Henderson, Miss Sprott, „
Cherrybank   do. ...Jas. Mackie, Miss Walker,   „
Craigend   do. ...Miss Mary L. Mason & Miss Jean Band

MUNRO MELVILL TRUST.

Governors—Bailie Law, Bailie Cunningham, Sir Samuel Chapman, John Dow, Rev. J. M'Glashan Scott. Joint Clerks—David Marshall and T. B. Marshall, solicitors.

EDUCATIONAL INSTITUTE OF SCOTLAND.

*Perthshire Branch.—*President, Hugh Leslie, F. E. I. S., Caledonian Road School; secretary, Mr. J. Purdie, B.A., Auchterarder; treasurer, Hugh Leslie, F.E.I.S., Caledonian Road School, Perth.

PROPERTY AND INCOME TAX.

GENERAL COMMISSIONERS.

The Sheriff-Substitute ex-officio is a commissioner in all the Districts.

PERTH DISTRICT.

The Lord Provost of Perth | The Dean of Guild of Perth
Alex. Macduff of Bonhard | Sir R. D. Moncreiffe, Bart.
Col. Smythe of Methven | R. W. R. Mackenzie

Robert Hunter, solicitor, Perth, clerk.
W. B. Rose, Tay Street, Perth, inspector and assessor

BLAIRGOWRIE DISTRICT

Sir James H. Ramsay of Bamff | *To supply vacancies*
Brig.-Gen. J. C. L. Campbell | Wm. Whitson, Esq., of Isla
of Achalader | Park
James Speid of Forneth | Ian S. M. Pender Small of
Robert R. Constable | Dirnanean.
Col. P. R. B. Clerk Rattray | *Additional Commissioners*
| F. Balfour, Esq., Kindrogan
| Wm. C. Macpherson, Blair-
| gowrie
| A. J. Meacher of Marlee

John B. Begg, Blairgowrie, clerk
T. C. Breen, Dundee, inspector and assessor

CARSE DISTRICT

James Drummond Hay of | The Earl of Moray
Seggieden | A. W. Cox of Glendoick
R. Wyllie Hill of Balthayock | Hon. A. D. Murray of Pitfour
Lord Kinnaird |

Charles P. Campbell, solictor, Perth, clerk
W. B. Rose, Perth, inspector and assessor

COUPAR-ANGUS DISTRICT

Wm. Whitson of Isla Park | *To supply vacancies.*
Sir George Kinloch, Bart. | William Dudgeon Graham
| Menzies of Hallyburton
| Col. W. Clark of Princeland
| J. M. Matthew of Auchmague,
| Balbeggie

Charles Boyd, solicitor, Coupar-Angus, clerk
T. C. Breen, Dundee, inspector and assessor

CRIEFF DISTRICT

Sir George W. M. Dundas, Bart. | Wm, Keith Murray
Sir P. K. Murray, Bart. | D. Keith Murray, Westerton
R. T. N. Spier of Culdees | Ochtertyre
John M'Nee, preserve manu- |
facturer, Crieff | *To supply vacancies*
A. G. Maxtone-Graham of | C. H. Graham Stirling of
Cultoquhey | Strowan
W. H. Mungall | G. T Ewing, Pitkellony

Malcolm Finlayson, solicitor, Crieff, clerk
W B. Rose, Perth, inspector and assessor

DUNBLANE DISTRICT

A. W. H. Hay Drummond of Cromlix

Brig.-Gen. Arch. Stirling of Keir

Jas. Richmond

John G. Stewart of Aultwharrie

John Stroyan of Lanrick.

Dr. T. W. Dewar

A. B. Wilson

To supply vacancies

Edmund Pullar

John A. Stirling of Kippendavie

Additional Commissioners

George Crabbie of Blairhoyle

Campbell Willison

James Templeton of Holmehill

General John H. Campbell

Fredk. C. Bishop

A. H. Anderson

James Barty, solicitor, Dunblane, clerk
A. Balfour Craig, Stirling, inspector and assessor

WEEM DISTRICT

The Marquis of Breadalbane, K.G.

John M. S. Steuart

Major John Scott of Eastertyre

Major J. S. Robertson of Edradynate

A. D. Stewart of Innerhadden

To supply vacancies

Charles J. D. Munro, solicitor, Aberfeldy, clerk
W. B. Rose, Perth, inspector and assessor

DUNKELD DISTRICT

W. T J. S. Steuart-Fothringham of Murthly

Albert E. Cox of Dungarthill

W H. Cox of Clunie & Snaigow

David Watson

The Duke of Atholl, K.T.

E. J. Fergusson of Baledmund

A. M. Meldrum, solicitor, Pitlochry, clerk
W. B. Rose, Perth, inspector and assessor

INCOME TAX.

INSPECTOR AND ASSESSOR FOR PERTHSHIRE
W. B. Rose, inspector.
Office—40 Tay Street, Perth
Surveyor's Clerks---H. L. Forbes, M. Scott,
W. D. Robertson, and D. R. Moir

CUSTOMS AND EXCISE, ALSO STAMPS AND TAXES.

A. J. Heatley, Collector and Distributor of Stamps
J. Casey, G. H. Lawrence, and P. P. Leyden, Surveyors.
H. D. Henderson; W. Caw, and C. Duigan. Officers.
E. Ince, J. Gyle, N. J. Cousins, E. Husband,
D. Brown, J. Fordyce.
W. H. Tanner, J. Shepherd, and W. A. Adie, Officers.
Office —40 Tay Street, Perth
John Kay, Collector of Customs and Excise, Stirling, Collector
for the Dunblane and Killin Districts, for Excise Duties only.

SUB-DISTRIBUTORS OF STAMPS

Aberfeldy	Post Office	Doune	Post Office
Alyth	Post Office	Dunblane	Post Office
Auchterarder	T. E. Young	Dunkeld	Post Office
Blairgowrie	J. B. Miller	Errol	Post Office
Callander	Post Office	Kincardine	Post Office
Coupar-Angus	Post Office	Pitlochry	Post Office
Crieff	Post Office		

VALUATION OF THE COUNTY 1920-1921.

UNDER THE NEW VALUATION ACT OF 1895-96

	£	s	d		£	s	d
Aberdalgie ...	5153	15	9	Kenmore	8645	19	2
Aberfoyle ...	8962	16	11	Killin	13081	8	2
Abernethy	12653	9	1	Kilmadock... ...	23229	17	11
Abernyte	2423	3	3	Kilspindie	5299	12	2
Alyth... ...	22418	1	6	Kincardine ...	14867	19	7
Ardoch	11587	1	4	Kinclaven	7682	19	1
Arngask ...	6866	4	3	Kinfauns	9596	11	9
Auchterarder ...	22590	4	4	Kinloch	3176	7	4
Auchtergaven ...	14644	15	8	Kinnaird	2873	10	8
Balquhidder ...	6374	13	4	Kinnoull	3011	11	8
Bendochy	9278	4	7	Kirkmichael ...	16889	0	5
Blackford	14861	7	9	Lethendy	2319	7	10
Blair-Atholl ...	18222	18	1	Little Dunkeld...	18779	13	0
Blairgowrie ...	33029	14	9	Logiealmond ...	5680	9	3
Callander ...	22548	17	2	Logierait	15935	3	6
Caputh ...	10527	14	0	Longforgan ...	15306	3	7
Cargill... ...	13855	18	8	Madderty	5325	9	10
Clunie... ...	7071	17	9	Meigle... ...	8377	2	1
Collace	3851	0	6	Methven	13038	17	3
Comrie ...	17998	13	6	Moneydie	3702	5	7
Coupar-Angus...	18337	5	7	Monzievaird & Strowan ...	9227	16	8
Crieff	52171	14	1				
Dron	3739	1	6	Moulin...	28825	19	2
Dull	20605	9	6	Muckhart	5642	12	4
Dunbarney ...	9145	0	5	Muthill	13544	6	7
Dunblane and Lecropt	39460	0	0	Perth (Landward)	2368	19	0
				Port of Monteith	11655	14	8
Dunkeld & Dowally	7684	13-	1	Rattray	12137	8	7
Dunning	12022	14	7	Redgorton... ...	11104	9	4
Errol	19158	14	2	Rhynd...	4491	1	10
Findo-Gask ...	4978	11	4	St. Madoes... ...	4599	2	6
Forgandenny ...	6920	15	0	St. Martins... ...	9500	2	8
Forteviot	7798	7	11	Scone	17463	18	11
Fortingall ...	20492	8	2	Tibbermore ...	11283	12	8
Fowlis-Wester...	13270	12	8	Trinity-Gask ...	5902	4	11
Glendevon... ...	7706	15	6	Weem	4291	17	11
Inchture	6837	5	0				

Total Rental of the County as made up by the Assessor of the County of Perth, ... £864,108 18 3

CHARLES CRAIG, Assessor.

RENTAL OF RAILWAYS AND WATERWORKS
IN COUNTY, 1920-1921

Caledonian Railway Company ...	...	£60,506 0 0
North British (including Strathendrick)	...	13,480 0 0
Highland...	...	6,008 0 0
Callander and Oban	...	9,489 0 0
Killin Railway	...	101 0 0
Forth and Clyde	...	......
Glasgow Corporation Water Works	...	29,674 0 0
Dunfermline Water Works ...	...	1,368 0 0
Dundee Water Works	...	4,855 0 0
Perth Corporation Tramways ...	...	374 0 0
Bankfoot Light Railway	...	......

Total £125,855 0 0

Assessor of Railways and Water Works—

R. JACKSON, Edinburgh

VALUATION OF THE CITY

Total Valuation for 1920-1921 ... ...£257,797 19 5

Whereof in the Parish of Perth   £220,533 9 7

    ,,   ,,   Kinnoull   25,284 8 8

    ,,   ,,   Scone   ...   11 6 0

    ,,   ,,   Tibbermore 11,968 15 2

                                —————£257,797 19 5

Unassessable Properties being—

    Churches, unlet premises, &c., £7142 4 6

Assessor—Donald Mackintosh, 12 Tay Street, Perth

Total Rental of Railways and Tramways in Burgh £14,577 0 0

Assessor—Robert Jackson, Edinburgh

COUNTY AND CITY ASSESSMENTS

COUNTY RATES—PERTH DISTRICT.

Branches of Expenditure and amount of Rate in the £
applicable to each

	Owners.	*Occupiers.*
1. Lands Valuation Expenses Rate ...	·192d	·150d
2. County Voters' Registration Expenses Rate	·404d	·350d
3. County General Assessment	·317d	·100d
4. Lunacy Assessment	1·187d	1·130d
5. Police Rate	2·439d	1·500d
6. Contagious Diseases (Animals) Rate...	·070d	·070d
7. General Purposes Rate, ...	·200d	·200d
8. Road Debt Assessment	·441d	--
9. Management and Maintenance of Highways Rate	21·000d	21·000d
10. Public Health General Expenses District Rate	1·500d	1·500d
	2/3·750d	2/2·000d

PERTH BURGH RATES.

Proprietors' Rates.

					Per Pound	
Poors Rates ...	...	...	...	...	0s	7·5
Sewer Rates ...	...	...	...	...	0s	2·875
Improvement ...	...	...	...	...	0s	2·625
Roads, &c. ...	...	...	...	...	0s	6·0
Burgh Rate and Minor Assessments	...	...			0s	7·5
Public Health ...	...	...	...	...	0s	4·0
School Rate ...	...	...	...	..	1s	1·6
Public Water Rate	...	...	...	...	0s	1·0
				Total	3/-	9·1

Tenants' Rates.

Poors Rates ...	...	...	...	...	0s	7·5
General, Police, Roads. Improvement, Public Health, Library Rate and Minor Assessments	...				4s	6·
Domestic Water Rate (Shops Half Rate),	...				0s	11·0
School Rate ...	...	...	...	...	1s	1·7
				Total	7/-	2·2

In the case of rents of and under £4 for Shops and £15 for Houses, the Tenants' Rates are levied from the landlords, the Acts allowing them to have recourse upon their tenants for the proportion of their respective rents.

POPULATION, INSPECTORS of POOR, & REGISTRARS OF EACH PARISH IN THE COUNTY.

Parishes and Registration District.	Population. 1911.	Inspectors of Poor.	Registrars.
Aberdalgie	278	Miss B. Forbes	B. Forbes
Aberf'dy (Burgh)	1592	———	Dond. Thomson
Aberfoyle	1147	John M'Intyre	John M'Intyre
Abernethy	1267	D. S. Mitchell	D. S. Mitchell
Abernyte	209	J. F. Falconer	J. F. Falconer
Alyth	2937	C. D. Mitchell	C. D. Mitchell
Ardoch	863	T. Blackwood	Wm. Monteith
Arngask	652	B. Murphie	Peter Anderson
Auchterarder	3175	Wm. M'Donald	Arch. M'Niven
Auchtergaven	2167	Arch. Naughton	A. Naughton
Balquhidder	664	D. M'Naughton	John M'Laren
Bendochy	542	Jas. Gibson	Jas. Gibson
Blackford	1374	John Stewart	Peter M. Gilmour
Blair-Atholl	1580	Geo. Forrest	Andw. Kellock
Blairgowrie	4319	Jas. S. Brown	Jas. S. Brown
Callander	2215	Jas. M'Donald	James M'Donald
Caputh	986	Jas. Ballantine	Jas. Ballantine
Cargill	1411	R. K. M'Intyre	Jas. S. Haliburton
Clunie	508	W. G. M'Gilchrist	W. G. M'Gilchrist
Collace	366	G. H. Dale	Geo. H. Dale
Comrie	1745	J. P. Mitchell	J. P. Mitchell
Coupar-Angus	2749	R. K. M'Intyre	R. K. M'Intyre
Crieff	6089	Pat. G. M'Ara	P. G. M'Ara
Doune (Burgh)	893	W. Gray	W. Gray
Dowally	—	G. Stewart	James Douglas
Dron	256	Miss M. S. Duff	Miss M. S. Duff
Dull	2361	James M'Donald	John Rhind
Dunbarney	862	J. Paul	John Ellis
D'blane & Lecr'pt	4591	J. C. Waddell	J. C. Waddell
Dunkeld and Dowally	1081	G. Stewart	G. Stewart
Dunkeld (Little)	2113	A. Harris	Chas. J. Low
Dunning	1145	W. Brown	W. Brown
Errol	2083	D. Nicoll	D. Nicoll
Findo-Gask	357	A. Wanless	A. Wanless
Forgandenny	540	A. C. Campbell	John Allan (jun.)
Forteviot	549	A. Wanless	Wm. Drummond
Fortingall	1524	R. Fisher	Jas. Simpson
Foss	—	———	Jessie Campbell
Fowlis-Wester	1007	J. R. Martin	J. R. Martin
Glendevon	148	W. N. Russell	W. N. Russell
Glenshee (dist.)	--		I. M. Sutherland

Parishesand Registration District	Population. 1911.	Inspectors of Poor.	Registrars.
Inchture	545	T. S. Nicolson	T. S. Nicolson
Innerwick, in Glenlyon	272	——	Thos. Connal
Kenmore	1106	John Rhind	Wm. Menzies
Killin	1412	Peter Stewart	Wm. Walker
Kilmadock	2428	William Gray	Wm. Gray
Kilspindie	498	Jno. M'Kellar	Jno. M'Kellar
Kincardine	1150	A. Paterson	John Meikle
Kinclaven	559	A. Robertson	J. Burnfield
Kinfauns	571	John Sprunt	John Sprunt
Kinloch	200	Jas. S. Brown	Geo. Elder
Kin.-Rannoch	787	——	Joseph M'Donald
Kinnaird	172	G. F. Duncan	Geo. F. Duncan
Kinnoull	3818	Robert Clark	R. Clark
Kirkmichael	816	Wm. Richmond	Wm. Richmond
Lecropt (See Dunblane)	—		
Lethendy	140	J. S. Brown	Geo. Elder
Logiealmond	489	Wm. Murray	Wm. Murray
Logierait	1618	W. A. M'Intosh	W. A. M'Intosh
Longforgan	1997	D. M. Boyd	D. M. Boyd
Madderty	438	R. Ironside	R. Ironside
Meigle	810	John Butter	John Butter
Methven	1847	Thos. Robertson	Thos. Robertson
Moneydie	237	A. L. Smith	Miss M. A. Young
Monivaird	508	A. Hill	A. Hill
Moulin	2670	R. H. Stewart	Jas. Finlay
Muckhart	535	David M. Hall	David M. Hall
Muthill	1269	P. G. M'Ara	A. Black
Persie	—		A. Croll (Int.)
Perth	30678	R. Stewart	James Bridges
Port of Monteith	1035	Peter Hay	John Kay
Rattray	2160	W. S. Neish	W. S. Neish
Redgorton	1462	A. L. Smith	Wm.K. Ardron
Rhynd	205	James Hay	James Hay
Scone	2341	W. G. M'Farlane	W. G. M'Farlane
Stanley	—	——	A. L. Smith
St. Madoes	359	John Leitham	John Leitham
St. Martins	820	J. C. Davidson	J. C. Davidson
Strathfillan	—	——	D. S. Black
Strathloch	—		Thomas Michie
Tenandry	—	——	Thos. M'Glashan
Tibbermore	2794	A. M. Dundas	A. M. Dundas
Trinity-Gask	360	Robert Brown	RobertBrown
Weem	439	James Morgan	Wm. M'Leish

NOTE.—The following parishes, partially in Perthshire, are wholly attached to the counties after-mentioned:—Arngask to the county of Fife; Coupar-Angus (excepting the estate of Kinloch, annexed to Meigle) to Forfar; Fossoway to Kinross; Kippen and Logie to Stirling.

Notice of a birth must be given to the Registrar within twenty-one days after its occurrence, and after three months no Registration can be made without a Sheriff's warrant.

Marriage. — The contracting parties must apply to the Registrar of the parish in which the marriage is to be solemnised, who, upon production of the Certificates of Proclamation or Publication, will issue marriage schedule. The schedule has to be returned to the Registrar within three days after the marriage.

Notice of a death must be given to the Registrar within eight days after the event.

FIARS PRICES—1891 to 1919.—Sterling Money.
The Fiars are per Quarter for Wheat, Barley, Oats, Pease, Rye —per Boll of 140 lbs. of Oatmeal.

Crop	Wheat best sort		Wheat 2nd sort		Barley best sort		Barley 2nd sort		Oats best sort		Oats 2nd sort		Pease		Rye		Meal	
	s	D	s	D	s	D	s	D	s	D	s	D	s	D	s	D	s	D
1891	36	3	32	3	28	7	21	2	22	4	20	8	32	6	34	10	14	10
1892	25	2	18	7	22	11	26	4	19	1	16	5	26	5	19	2	17	4
1893	24	2	22	6	25	11	17	0	18	5	17	1	28	3	18	9	17	7
1894	20	6	17	8	21	5	23	7	16	8	14	10	24	2	17	1	15	7
1895	23	2	21	8	20	3	17	—	15	7	14	—	26	6	18	3	14	11
1896	27	7	24	3	21	6	17	7	15	6	13	9	25	7	15	9	13	—
1897	33	5	28	10	26	10	16	1	18	10	16	8	28	11	18	8	14	—
1898	26	9	25	4	26	9	22	10	18	1	16	5	29	6	18	4	15	11
1899	27	0	23	6	24	10	23	10	16	7	14	9	28	8	19	7	14	3
1900	26	10	24	1	23	9	23	10	18	8	16	6	30	4	19	10	14	10
1901	27	4	25	—	25	3	20	7	20	6	17	11	33	3	21	1	15	8
1902	27	3	21	10	23	7	22	6	19	—	15	11	31	5	20	6	15	5
1903	27	1	22	9	21	—	19	—	16	4	11	2	—	—	17	7	15	3
1904	28	11	24	8	24	11	13	7	17	10	15	10	28	2	20	3	15	5
1905	27	7	25	9	24	5	22	7	17	11	16	7	31	11	21	1	14	8
1906	25	5	24	—	23	7	22	11	18	6	16	5	31	3	20	2	14	6
1907	32	3	23	8	25	—	21	8	20	8	15	—	34	—	23	6	14	6
1908	30	10	26	4	27	—	18	3	18	5	16	2	31	11	21	5	17	9
1909	33	5	28	11	27	10	23	5	18	11	16	7	32	1	20	7	15	7
1910	30	2	27	—	23	9	23	5	16	9	15	8	31	10	20	1	15	—
1911	32	10	30	8	34	9	21	5	20	6	18	4	38	1	24	2	16	—
1912	33	5	31	—	32	—	29	—	21	8	19	7	—	—	25	2	16	2
1913	29	3	26	9	27	—	22	5	19	8	18	—	30	10	20	1	16	1
1914	43	—	—	—	32	4	26	11	27	4	22	7	42	—	30	9	20	2
1915	53	8	—	—	49	—	47	—	30	5	27	3	—	—	43	5	24	8
1916	65	—	—	—	67	—	60	—	46	—	35	—	76	11	53	4	33	2
1917	75	3	—	—	66	—	62	9	52	—	46	3	113	—	80	—	38	10
1918	75	—	—	—	69	6	67	3	53	3	49	7	118	1	75	7	41	0
1919	75	—	—	—	110	9	103	2	62	—	57	6	110	10	77	9	47	—

ESTABLISHED CHURCH MINISTERS

Of the several Parishes within the bounds of the Presbytery of Perth from the Reformation to the present time, with the date of their incumbencies.

ABERDALGIE

1567-72 William Melrose	1718-44 James Mercer
1594- Patrick Wemyss	45-81 Thomas Rankin
1613-58 Andrew Playfair	82-1831 William Garvie
59-62 George Halyburton	1832-43 Charles C. Stewart
63-67 Mungo Weemyss	43-46 Maitland Thomson
68-76 David Lauder	46-87 John Sharp
77-78 David Moncrieff	81-1911 J. Ferguson, M.A.,
79-90 John Hardie	B.D.
1691-1718 David Schaw	1911-18 J. Macfarlane, B.D.

1919 Rev. R. S. V. Logie, M.A.

ABERNETHY

1567 Patrick Galt	1780-1809 William Duncan
1585 Patrick Wemyss	1809-62 David Duncan
1586-1629 Archibald Moncrieff	62-65 Archibald Scott
1630-71 Arch. Moncrieff, jun.	65-70 David Miller
72-90 Robert Jenkins	71-90 William Gordon
91-1719 Alexander Dunning	90-1902 Dugald Butler, M.A.
1720-40 Alexander Moncrieff	1903 George M'Dougall, B.D.
1747-79 Andrew Gray	

COLLACE

1569 James Anderson	1774-77 Hamilton Kilgour
82-96 Henrie Guthrie	78-83 John Baird
96-1618 Patrick Smith	83-1812 William M'Leish
1619 Patrick Smyth	1800-51 John Rodgers
1620-31 Andrew Forester	38-43 Andrew Bonar, A.S.
32-70 William Halyburton	44-51 James Laing, A.S.
70-89 George M'Gruther	52-55 Thomas Leishman
92-1709 James Campbell	55-1901 Thomas Brown
1709-12 John Smith	1901-07 Geo. Nisbet Dods, M.A.
13-39 James Ramsay	08 Geo. Veitch, M.A.
40-73 John Faichney	

DRON

1586-92 Patrick Wemyss	1698-1726 John Colquhoun
93-1603 Alex. Justice	1727-31 Thomas Tullidelph
1605-41 Patrick Rhynd	. 41-56 Robert Bryce
41-52 William Bell	58-1808 David Dow
53-53 William Wemyss	1807-34 Alexander Isdale
56-80 Alexander Pitcairn	36-44 Patrick J. M'Farlane
82-90 Thomas Taylor	44-98 Charles Goodall
90-91 Alexander Pitcairn	97 W. A. Shepherd
1692-96 John Adie	

DUNBARNEY

1567   Patrick Wemyss
1615-22 William Black
 23-46 John Hall
 47-64 Robert Young
 65-75 John Wemyss
 76-79 John Omay
 79-80 David Anderson
 81-89 John Balneavis
 91-1714 John Tullidelph

1717-44 Thomas Finlayson
 46-50 James Lindsay
 51-57 James Gillespie
 59-95 David Beatson
 95-1820 James Beatson
1821-33 John Anderson, D.D.
 34-43 Alexander Cumming
 43-93 Thomas D. Kirkwood
 93   J. S. Clark, M.A.

ERROL

1569 Alex. Allardyce
 71 Alex. Dunmore
 81 James Smith
1614-26 John Strang
 26-39 Alexander Omay
 40-48 Thomas Halyburton
 52-65 William Bell
 66-90 John Nicholson
 92-1720 Samuel Nairne
1725-44 Lachlan Macintosh

 44-58 James Wemyss
 59-94 James Jobson
 95-1818 David Dow
1818-43 James Grierson
 43-49 William Turnbull
 49-57 John Caird
 58-1900 Robt. Graham, LL.D.
1900-14 Robert Coupar, B.D.
1914   K. D. Maclaren

FORGANDENNY

1567-72 William Lauder
 73-88 John Row
 89-1624 William Row
1624-58 William Row, A.S.
 60-62 David Orme
 63-67 John Liddel
 67-90 Andrew Hardie
 95-1702 William Dick
1703-40 Peter Pilmar

1741-92 John Glen
 93-1828 John Willison
1828-43 James Drummond
 43-61 John Wilson
 61-65 John Pagan
 66-67 James Johnston
 68-75 David Williamson
 75-1909 John T. Robb
1909   J. P. Brownlie

PORTEVIOT

1591   John Clerk
 93-99 Colin Rhynd
1602-34 James Ross
 35-49 Edward Richardson
 51-90 William Barclay
 90-96 Vacant
 96-97 Alexander Chalmers
 99-1703 Andrew Harlaw
1707-9 James Walker

1711-18 James Mercer
 20-33 James Mackie
 36-51 Alexander Mair
 52-99 Harry Inglis
1800-22 William Henderson
 22-56 R. J. Robertson
 57-1902 Jas. Anderson, D.D.
1903-10 James Kirk, M.A.
1910-16 J. W. Oastler. B.D.
1917   Neil Meldrum, B.D.

KILSPINDIE

1563   Alex. Jardine
 67   Alex. Dunmuir
 87-1614 James Row
1615-22 George Symer
 22-46 David Williamson

1646-56 John Hall
 56-65 Henry Guthrie, afterwards Bishop of Dunkeld
 67-91 John Blair
 98-1726 William English

1727-61 Robert Coventry
62-87 Alan Stewart
89-1818 Anthony Dow

1818-50 David Black
50-93 W. L. Wotherspoon
88   J. M. Strachan, B.D.

KINFAUNS

1568   Wm. Edmestoun
95-1610 Robert Ramsay
1611-1623 Alex. Bruce
23-67 James Foular
67-87 John Murray
87-97 John Gall
1700-12 Matthew Coupar
14-31 Robert Lyon
32-58 Charles Phut
59-62 James Scott

1763-64 John Nimmo
65-95 George Chapman
97-1816 John Duff
1816-21 Robert Gordon
21-43 James MacLaggan
43-52 Lachlan M'Lean
53-1901 George S. Davidson.
        M.A.
94   Roger S. Davidson.
        B.D.

KINNOULL

1568-1610 William Rhynd
1611-35 Ninian Drummond
35-40 Thomas Hallyburton
40-65 James Oliphant
65-97 Thomas Foular
98-1731 Andrew Darling
1733-45 Thomas Rankin

1746-60 Patrick Bannerman
61-82 Patrick Meek
82-1829 Lewis Dunbar
1829-52 Edward Touch
52-96 John Anderson, D.D.
97   J. W. Henderson, B.D.

LOGIEALMOND

1854-58 Adam Milroy
1859-99 P. M'Gregor, M.A., PH. D.

1900-04 W. B. Kennedy, B.D.
1904-15 G. Miller, B.D.
1916   James Grieve.

METHVEN

1567-72 Alex. Young
73   James Heron
93   John Young
1607-1614 William Buchanan
15-48 Robert Murray
48-62 John Murray, A.S.
62-79 Hugh Ramsay
79-92 John Omay

1694-1748 William Moncrieff
1750-83 James Oswald, D.D.
84-1823 John Dowe
1824-41 Thomas Clark, D.D.
41-59 Thos. Buchanan, D.D.
1859-1904 John Wilson, M.A.
1904   James Robertson,
        D.D., D.S.O.

MONEYDIE

1568-96 Thomas Makgibbon
96-1626 Alexander Omay
1626-49 Patrick Omay
1755-78 David Drummond
79-90 William Smyth
01-2   James Fleming
2-16 Alexander Chapman
17-38 John Gardiner

1739-54 Gilbert Mann
54-61 Patrick Meek
62-1807 George Fraser
1807-27 James Somerville
28-43 John W. Thomson
43-58 Robert T. Auld
58-99 Adam Milroy, D.D.
99   D. G. Young, B.D.

PERTH

First Minister

1560-80 John Row
  81-89 Patrick Galloway
  91-1634 John Malcolm
1634-45 John Robertson
  45-52 Alexander Rollock
  55-62 William Colville
  62-67 Harrie Auchinleck
  68-79 Wm. Lindsay (Bishop
      of Dunkeld)

1679-79 Alexander Skeen
  79-88 David Anderson
  91-1704 Robert Anderson
1705-11 George Blair
  13-19 John Fleming
  21-33 William Stewart
  37-71 David Black
  73-1807 James Moodie

Second Minister

1595-1615 Wm. Coupar (Bishop
      of Galloway)
1617-19 John Guthry (Bishop
      of Moray)
  22-34 John Robertson
  35-40 Joseph Lawrie
  41-44 Robert Lawrie (Bishop
      of Brechin)
  44-64 George Hallyburton
      (Bishop of Dunkeld)
  65-71 Mungo Low

1672-79 Alex. Ross (Bishop o
      Moray)
  84-88 William Hay (Bishop
      of Moray)
  88-88 Adam Barclay
  98-1739 Thomas Black
1741-45 Henry Lindsay
  47-55 John Warden
  56-62 John Bonnar
  62-1807 James Scott
  73-1807 John Duff, assistant

Third Minister

1713 William Wilson (left with the Seceders of 1733)

East Church

1808-10 And. Thomson, D.D.
  10-44 James Esdaile, D.D.
  45-52 John Anderson, M.A.
  52-59 James Elder Cumming

1860-62 Archibald Scott, M.A.
  63-70 James A. Burden
  71-1902 W. G. H. Carmichael, M.A.
1901 Walter E. Lee, M.A.

West Church

1807-13 Daniel Mackenzie
  03-19 Robert Keay
  19-35 Samuel Kennedy
  36-43 Andrew Gray

1843-45 Edward Robertson
  46-56 David Smith
  57-95 Robert Milne, D.D.
  95   P. R. Landreth

Middle Church

1808-43 W. A. Thomson, D.D.
  43-74 John Murdoch
  74-82 J. Brunton, M.A., B.D.

1882-91 W. Stevenson, M.A.
  92-1902 Wm. Main
1902 J. M'Glashan Scott, M.A.

St. Paul's Church

1807-46 John Findlay, D.D.
  46-50 Wm. Henry Gray
1850-56 Alex. Falconer
1856-1900 Arch. Fleming, B.A.

1900-12 F. H. Martin, B.D.
1912-14 M. Stewart, B.D.
1915-18 J. Wilson, M.A.
1918   J. Mackenzie, M.A.

St. Andrew's Church

1885-1908 D. G. Manuel, B.D. | 1908-18 C. Robertson, M.A.
1919 Rev. John Freeland, M.A.

St. Leonard's Church

1862-88 James Wilson | 1888 J. S. Macnaughton

St. Stephen's Church

1896-1910 R. Oswald, B.D. | 1910-20 A. Moffatt, B.D.
                           1920   John Strathern, M A.

St. Mark's Chapel—1905-18 R. S. Barclay

REDGORTON

1574-1625 Andrew Colt
1614-25 William Young
26-62 John Cruikshank
65-81 James Carnegie
82-91 Patrick Auchterlony
1700-10 George Blackie
13-56 George Meek

1756-62 George Fraser
63-1811 David Moncrieffe
1812-64 William Liston
65-97 Alex. Neilson
98-09 A. M. Snadden, B.D.
1910-15 H. D. Swan, B.D.
1916 David Graham

RHYND

1591 John Wood
1628-31 John Wood, yr.
32-44 Alex. Petrie
45-66 James Gillespie
66-67 John Smythe
68-77 Gabriel Semple
78-96 William Paplay
99-1721 Thomas Fisher

1722-29 Francis Ferguson
31-61 John Moncrieff
62-1814 William Taylor
1814-41 James Traquhair, ▲.s.
41-44 John Struthers, ▲.s.
47-77 Richard Ramsay
77 J. Ballingall, D.D.

ST. MADOES

1574-90 David Balvaird
1591-1639 Alexander Lindsay,
Bishop of Dunkeld
1640-67 James Campbell
68-76 John Omay
76-87 George Drummond
88-97 Thomas Hall
99-1701 John Drummond
1701-6 George Blair
06-21 John Dempster
22-27 Robert Watson

1729-40 Andrew Shaw
41-46 Patrick Bannerman
47-84 Archibald Stevenson,
85-94 David Black
95-1828 Thomas Kennedy
1828-48 James Noble
49-56 John R. Macduff
56-1903 Walter Tait
1904-12 A. Main, M.A.
1912-19 W. W. D. Gardiner.
1920— J. H. Duncan, M.A.,
B.Phil.

ST. MARTINS

15- T. Strachan
1601-43 John Straquhan
43-71 Thomas Straquhan
72-76 Patrick Straquhan
77-81 James Inglish
95-1710 George Jamieson
1712-47 James Faichney
48-57 Alexander Badenoch

1758-1810 David Bannerman
1802-36 Wm. Constable, ▲.s.
36-38 Peter Curror
38-43 William Ritchie, D.D.
44-65 John Park
65-98 W. M. S. Hamilton
96 Alex. I. Scott, B.D.

SCONE

1567 Thos. Morrison
84 John Abercrombie
1601-3 George Graham, who
became Bishop or Brechin
18 Carmichael or Fyffe
20-64 David Wemys
56-66 George Wemys, ▲.s.
67-86 John Liddell
87-90 John Murray
1698-1701 William Chrystie
1707-8 James Stewart
09-45 Thomas Schaw

1748-54 David Craigie
54-76 James Knox
77-81 Charles Wilson
82-93 James Hunter
93-94 John Wright
95-1832 William Aitken
1832-43 James Craik
44-72 John Crombie, D.D.
73-94 Andrew Benvie, B.D.
94-1908 A. Stuart Martin, B.D.
1908 D. L. Blair, B.D.

STANLEY

1822 R. J. Johnston	1877-93 George Murray
32-43 Wm. Mather	88-17 W. C. Malcolm
	1917- N. F. Orr, B.A., B.D.

TIBBERMORE

1501 Patrick Murray	1741-61 Patrick Duncan,
1572 Alex. Young	62-85 Alexander Duff
1618 John Murray	86-99 John Inglis
18-40 Alexander Balneavis	1800-31 Thomas Taylor D.D.
40-92 Alexander Balneavis	33-45 Weir Tulloch
73-81 John Balneavis, A.S.	45-68 Edward Robertson
81-87 Alex. Balneavis, A.S.	68-93 Charles Smith Adie
94-1741 David Meldrum	94-16 Harry Smith, M.A.
	1916 James C. Campbell, M.A.

MINISTERS IN PERTH AND SCONE.

Rev. Walter E. Lee, M.A., East Church.............. seated for 750
J. M'Glashan Scott, M.A., Middle .... „ 1208
P. R. Landreth, West .... „ 800
Jas. Mackenzie, M.A., St. Paul's .... „ 1000
J. S. Macnaughton, St. Leonard's.......... ... „ 991
John Freeland, M.A., St. Andrew's............. „ 750
John Strathern, M.A., St. Stephen's............. „
St. Mark's .... „ 530
John W. Henderson, B.D., Kinnoull............ „ 750
David Logan Blair, B.D., Scone . ... „ 550
D. W. Kennedy, and
J. Westland Rose, Middle United Free ...... „ 830
P. A. Gordon Clark, West United Free...... „ 950
J. U. Macgregor, M.A., St. Leonard's U.F. ... „ 1000
Joseph Shillinglaw, B.D., St. Stephen's U.F. „ 850
Chas. Walls, M.A., St. Paul's United Free „ 600
Fergus Ferguson, B.D., North do. .... „ 1200
David R. M. Keir, M.A., Wilson do. .... „ 831
Thomas Crawford, B.D.,
and J. D. Lindsay, M.A., East do. ...... „ 672
Rev. Wm. Paterson, B.D., York Place do. „ 800
A. B. Macdonald, B.D., Bridgend United Free „ 500
Mr. Calder, Knox Free Church.................. „ 600
John W. Slater, B.D., West U.F., Scone „ 400
William M. Mathieson, B.D., Abbey United
Free Church, Scone,.............................. „ 400
Mr. Calder, Free Church. Scone .... „ 100
Right Rev. Charles E. Plumb, D.D., Bishop of St. ⎫
Andrews ; Provost—The Very Rev. P. M. ⎬ St. Ninian's
Smythe, M.A. .... ⎭ Cathedral
Rev. G. T. S. Farquhar, M.A., Oxon, Precentor ⎰ 1000
J. G. Miller, W.S., Chapter Clerk ....
Rev. G. R. Vallings, M.A., St. John's Episcopal...seated for 600
R. R. Hobart, M.A., Original Seceders......... „ 390
E. A. Evans, Wesleyan Methodist. .... „ 400
J. A. G. Robinson, M.A., Baptist Chapel...... „ 1200
Robert Finlay and
Congregational .... „ 420
Rev. John McDaniel. Rev. Joseph Cassidy,
Catholic Chapel.................................. „ 500
Very Rev. John Bullen (Rector), St. Mary's, Kinnoull.

CLERKS OF CHURCH COURTS.—CHURCH OF SCOTLAND.

Synod of Perth and Stirling	Rev. D. G. Young, B.D., Moneydie, Perth
Dunkeld Presbytery............	„ T. R. Rutherford M.A., Dunkeld
Weem Presbytery...............	„ W. A. Macfarlane, Dull, Aberfeldy
Perth „	„ D. G. Young, B.D., Moneydie, Perth
Auchterarder „	„ D. J. Maclaren, M.A., Trinity Gask, Auchterarder
Stirling „	„ Arch. Miller, M.A., Stirling (West)
Dunblane „	„ D. R. Henderson, Lecropt, Bridge of Allan.

UNITED FREE CHURCH OF SCOTLAND

Synod of Perth and Stirling	Rev. J. E. M'Ouat, B.D., Logie-almond, Perthshire
Stirling & Dunblane „	„ G. W. S. Cowie, Buchlyvie, Stirling
Breadalbane Presbytery........	„ W. H. Tulloch, Fortingall, Aberfeldy
Blairgowrie „	„ J. F. Linn, M.A., Airlie, Kirriemuir
Perth „	„ J. W. Slater, B.D., Scone
Auchterarder „	„ W. Hall, Comrie
Dunfermline & Kinross „ ...	„ Wm. Forbes, Cairneyhill, Dunfermline „ J. W. Duncan, M A., Lassodie, Dunfermline

EPISCOPAL CHURCH IN SCOTLAND.
UNITED DIOCESE OF ST. ANDREWS, DUNKELD AND DUNBLANE

Comprising the Counties of Fife, Kinross, Clackmannan, Perth (excluding Carse of Gowrie), and part of Forfar.

Bishop—Right Rev. Charles E. Plumb, D.D.

Dean—The Very Rev. George T. S. Farquhar, M.A., Perth. Synod Clerk—Rev. Canon Meredith, M.A. Diocesan Inspector of Schools—Rev. Canon Vallings, M.A. Diocesan Registrar—J. G. Miller, W.S. Diocesan Auditor—*vacant*.

Diocesan Supernumerary—Vacant. Chancellor—E. T. Neish. Sheriff Substitute, Dundee. Hon. Secy., W. T. Farquhar, Forfar.

CATHEDRAL OF THE UNITED DIOCESE, ST. NINIAN'S, PERTH.—*Residentiary Clergy.*

Provost—Very Rev. Patrick M Smythe, M.A., Braco, Perth. Dean and Precentor—Very Rev. G. T. S. Farquhar, M.A., 31 Barossa Place. *Canon and Chancellor*—Rev. J. Cunnynghame M.A. Chaplain—Vacant.

Non-residentiary: Canons—Rev. C. J. K. Bowstead, M.A., Blair-Atholl; Rev. J. A. Philip, M.A., Kirriemuir; Rev. W. M. Meredith, M.A. Crieff; Rev. J. W. Harper, M.A., Culross; Rev. J. Vallings, D.S.O., Perth; Rev. Gordon W. Paterson, M.A., Cupar.

Lay Elector—Sir R. D. Moncreiffe, Bart. *Lay Representative*—
F. Norie-Miller, Esq. *Hon. Secy. and Treas.*—W. H. Philips,
Somerset, Perth. *Asst. Secy.*—R. Pinkerton. *Chapter Clerk*—
J. G. Miller. W.S., 10 Blackfriars St. *Organist*—S. Richardson,
Barossa Pl. *Cathedral School, Head-mistress*—Miss Keith.
(Infants: Miss Bryce.)

CATHOLIC CHURCHES AND PRIESTS
IN PERTHSHIRE.

Aberfeldy,	Attended from Strathtay
Auchterarder,	Attended from Crieff.
Alyth,	Attended from Blairgowrie.
Blairgowrie,	Rev Walter R. Stretch.
Crieff,	Rev. Joseph Keenan.
Doune,	Very Rev. Canon Dowling.
Dunblane,	Attended from Doune.
Dunkeld (Birnam),	Attended from Strathtay.
Perth, { St. John's,	Rev. John McDaniel.
	Rev. Joseph Cassidy.
St. Mary's Kinnoull,	Very Rev. John Bullen (Rector),
Pitlochry,	Attended from Strathtay
Stanley,	Attended from Perth
Strathtay	Rev. John Coogan

LIST OF SOLICITORS IN THE CITY AND COUNTY.

Those marked thus * are Notaries Public.

PERTH.

Anderson, Walter
Bates, R. Martin
Begg, J.
*Bowie, J. Lyall
Boyes, Peter G.
*Buik, P. R , W.S.
Burt, W. C.
Cameron, J. C.
Campbell, A. C.
Campbell, Charles P.
Campbell John,
*Campbell, Robert
Coates, D. A.;
Cram, Duncan.
Dempster, Thomas
Douglas, G. R. P.
Douglas, J. T.
Forrest, A, G.
Glass, D.
Gordon, C. H.
*Gray, G. N.
Gray, W.
Hunter, A. D.
*Hunter, Robert
Hunter, W. N. G. ·
*Kippen, Robert M.
Little, John

Logan, Thomas
*Mackay, David M.
*Mackay, D.
Mackenzie, David,W.S.
M'Nab, Duncan
M'Pherson, Thomas
Marshall, David
*Marshall, T. B.
Miller, Andrew
*Miller, George A., W.S.
Miller, J. G.
*Mitchell, James
*Mitchell, J. W. Rollo
Munro, William
*Pinkerton, Robert
Purves, George
*Robertson, James
*Sneddon, A. M.
Stewart, Alexander
Stewart, Robert
*Strang, Peter
Taylor, E. N.
*Thomas, J. Hill
Turpie, James
Wyllie, J. W.
—— Young, W. Cochrane
Young. A. H.

ABERFELDY.

Clow, Andrew
*Kippen, R. M.
Munro, C. J. D.

ALYTH.

*Ferguson. A. M.
*Kidd, D. S.
Smith, W. R.
*Yeaman, John

AUCHTERARDER.

Kennaway, J. P.
M'Beth, J.
M'Farlane, J.
*M'Farlane, P. H.
*Young, T. E., W.S.

BLACKFORD.

M'Beth, J.

BLAIRGOWRIE.

Begg, J. B.
*Black, R. R.
Hodge, J. M.
*Keay, William
*Miller, J. B.
*Noble, J. P.
Stewart, J.
Young, J. W.

CALLANDER.

*Buchanan, Peter
*M'Laren, Donald
M'Michael, John

COMRIE.

Mickel, S. G.
Mitchell, J. P.

COUPAR-ANGUS.

Adam, John
*Boyd, Charles
*Watson, R.

CRIEFF.

Campbell, A. C.
Colville, C. E.
*Drysdale, S.
*Finlayson, M.
M'Duff, Thomas
*MacRosty, J.
Mickel, S. G.
Reid, James
Ross, Charles D. M.

DOUNE.

M'Lean, John A.

DUNBLANE.

Barty, A. B.
Barty, J. ...
M'Lean, J. A.
*Stewart, J.

DUNKELD.

M'Gillewie, R.

ERROL.

Graham, F. B.
*Melville, L.

KILLIN:

Clow, Andrew
Munro, C. J. D.

PITLOCHRY.

Gordon, C. H.
*Liddell, B. W., W.S.
*Macbeth, A.
*Meldrum, A. M.
*Mitchell, H.
M'Nab, D.

TERRITORIAL FORCE ASSOCIATION OF THE COUNTY OF PERTH.

President—Atholl, Col, (Bt. Maj. and temporary Brig.-Gen. in the Army) J. G., Duke of, K.T., C.B., M.V.O., D.S.O., Scottish Horse (Scouts), (Lord Lieutenant).

Chairman—Moncrieffe, Col. Sir R. D, Bart., C.M.G., V.D., A.D.C., Territorial Force, Hon. Colonel 6th Bn. Royal Highlanders

Vice-Chairman—Scrymsoure-Steuart-Fothringham, Lt.-Col. W. T. J., T.F. Res. Scottish Horse (Vice-Lieutenant).

Military Members--

Lyle, Major, A.M.P., M.C., Scottish Horse (Scouts).
Dewar, Major The Hon. J., M.C., Scottish Horse (Scouts).
Gibson, Major L., D.S.O., T.D., 6th Bn. The Black Watch.
MacRosty, Capt. J., 6th Bn. The Black Watch.
Cairncross, Major J. C., 6th Bn. The Black Watch
Stirling, Lt.-Col. R. M.D., T.D., R.A.M C. (T.F.)
Gray, Major W., D.S.O., 51st (The Highland) Divisional Train, R.A.S.C., (T.F.)
Scrymsoure-Steuart-Fothringham, Lt.-Col. W. T. J., T. F. Res. Scottish Horse (Vice-Lieutenant).
Henderson, Colonel, H.D., D.S O., V.D., T.D., Territorial Force, 51st (The Highland) Divisional Train, R.A.S.C.
Pullar, Major H. S., T.F. Reserve, Scottish Horse (Hon. Lieut. in Army).
Dawson, Lieut.-Col., R.G., Scottish Horse (Scouts).

Representative Members.

County Council.

Boyd, C., Esq.
Mansfield, A. D., Earl of, D.L.
Smythe, Col. D. M., late 3rd Bn. Royal Highlanders.
Steuart, Capt. J. M. S., late Scottish Horse.
Stirling, Lt.-Col. A., T. F. Reserve, 2nd Lovat Scouts (Maj. ret. pay) (Reserve of Officers).

Burgh of Perth.

Wotherspoon, A.U., Esq.

Co-opted Members.

Moncrieffe, Col. Sir Robert D., Bart., C.M.G., V.D., A.D.C., 6th Bn. The Black Watch.
Wylie, Lieut-Col. J., T.D., T.F. Res., late 6th Bn. Royal Highlanders.
M'Kenzie, W. H., late R.Q.M.S., 6th Bn. Royal Highlanders.
Young, James, late Sgt. Scottish Horse (Scouts).
Secretary—Little, Capt. J., T.F. Res., 10 Blackfriars Street, Perth. Regd. tel. address. "Territory," Perth, Tel No. 360.

Units administered by the Association.

Scouts—Scottish Horse (Scouts). -
Infantry—6th Bn. Royal Highlanders.
Royal Army Service Corps—51st (The Highland) Divisional Train, R.A.S.C.
Royal Army Veterinary Corps—1st -Scottish Veterinary Hospital.

POST OFFICE.

R. W. CRAWFORD, Postmaster; A. RUTHERFORD, Superintendent.

DESPATCH OF LETTER MAILS FROM PERTH.

(Head Office or Sorting Office).   Box Closes.

Alyth, Blairgowrie, Coupar-Angus, Meigle, and Stanley, Auchterarder, Blackford, Braco, Crieff, Dunblane, Dunning, Forgandenny, Glasgow (including part of Ireland, South and West of Scotland), and Stirling, Dunfermline, Edinburgh (South and East of Scotland), Kelty, Kinross, Milnathort, and West Riding of Yorkshire, ...   **5.0 a.m.**

Fife, generally (including Cupar, Kirkcaldy, Ladybank, and St. Andrews, Bankfoot, Glasgow (except Monday), Dundee, Aberdeen and Highland Lines (all places), Abernethy, Bridge of Earn, Glenfarg and Newburgh, Redgorton, Errol, Glencarse, and Inchture—First Town Delivery, ...   **6.0 a.m.**

Almondbank, Glenalmond, Logiealmond, South generally (important English Mail), Aberdeen (except Monday), Crieff, Dundee, Edinburgh, Glasgow, also East, South, and South-West of Scotland, and most of Ireland—Rural delivery, ...   **7.30 a.m.**

Town Delivery—Aberdeen, Arbroath, Brechin, Dundee, Elgin, Forfar, Forres, Glasgow, Grantown-on-Spey, Inverness, Montrose, Nairn, Pitlochry, South-West of Scotland, Stonehaven, and most of Ireland; South, generally (moderate English Mail), ...   **10.45 a.m.**

Edinburgh, ...   **11.45 a.m.**

Dundee, Kirkcaldy, Kinross, Milnathort, ...   **12.15 p.m.**

Auchterarder, Crieff, and Stirling, ...   **12.45 p.m.**

Glasgow, including South and South-West of Scotland, and part of Ireland, ...   **2.0 p.m.**

Aberdeen, Alyth, Blairgowrie, Coupar-Angus, Dundee, Forfar, Meigle, Montrose, Edinburgh, also South-East of Scotland, and North-East of Scotland, and North-East of England, ...   **2.30 p.m.**

Aberfeldy, Almondbank, Bankfoot, Bridge of Earn, Dunkeld, Errol, Glencarse, Glenfarg, Meikleour, Methven, Murthly, Pitlochry, Stanley, and Fife, ...   **3.0 p.m.**

3rd Town and part Rural delivery, ...   **3.30 p.m.**

Edinburgh, Glasgow, Dundee, Stirling, Inchture, Dunning, Forgandenny, and Scone; South, generally (important English Mail), ...   **4 p.m.**

St. Andrew's (except Saturday), ...   **5.0 p.m.**

Dundee and part of Fife, Aberdeen, ...   **6.15 p.m.**

Dunfermline, Edinburgh, Leeds, Newcastle-on-Tyne, Nottingham, and York, Inverness (Saturday only),   ...   **6.45 p.m.**
Falkirk, Glasgow, Greenock, and Ireland, ...

Dundee and Aberdeen, ...   **7.30 p.m.**

London, East and West Coast of England, and Ireland, ...   **8.0 p.m.**

Edinburgh and Glasgow, ...   **8.45 p.m.**

Aberdeen Line, Highland Line, Dundee, Fife, Stirling, and Glasgow, ...   **11.0 p.m.**

SUNDAY.

London, Edinburgh, Glasgow, Stirling, and South, all England, and Ireland, ...   **2.0 p.m.**

Registered Letters should be handed in at the Public Counter at least 30 minutes before the closing of the box for ordinary correspondence at the Head Office.

Deliveries—1st delivery, 7.15 a.m. (Parcels, 8.45 a.m.) ; 2nd delivery, 11.30 a.m , 3rd, 4.15 p.m. Sunday callers delivery, 9.30 a.m. to 10.30 a.m. Poste Restante, at Head Office ; Private Box Holders, and Express Service at Sorting Office.

The Office is open from 8 a.m. to 7 p.m. Sundays, 9 to 10.30 a.m.

Money-Order, Savings Bank, Insurance, and Annuity business during office hours.

EXPRESS DELIVERY SERVICE.

A fee of 6d a mile is charged from the Office (Telegraph) of delivery to the address for such services in addition to the postage of letters, etc., posted at an office where transmission by postmen or mail is entailed.

INLAND LETTERS AND PACKETS.

The rate of postage on all inland letters is regulated by weight, irrespective of distance, and is as follows, if paid in advance :—

Letter not exceeding 3 oz. in weight, 2d ; and ½d for every additional 1 oz.

Dimensions—2 feet in length by 1 in width, or 1 in depth.

NEWSPAPERS.

Every registered newspaper, whether posted singly or with others in a parcel. not exceeding 6 oz., 1d ; for every additional 6 oz., ½d.

Limits—weight 2 lbs., size 2 feet long by 1 wide, or 1 deep.

MAGAZINE POST.

Registered Magazines are forwarded to Canada and Newfoundland by Sea Route only.

MAGAZINE POST FOR CANADA AND NEWFOUNDLAND.

For each packet over 2 oz. but not over 6 oz. –1d.
  do.   do.   6 oz.   do.   1½ lbs —1½d.
  do.   do.   1½ lbs.   do.   2 lbs.--2d
  do.   do.   2 lbs.   do.   2½ lbs—2½d.

And ½d for every additional ½ lb. up to 5 lbs.

Maximum weight, 5 lbs.

Packets less than 2 oz. in weight are charged at the Printed Paper Rate.

HALFPENNY PACKETS.

Not more than 1 oz. ...   .   ½d

Weighing not more than 2 oz. 1d

    ½d. every additional 2 oz. up to limit of 2 lbs.

Typewritten (or imitation) circulars in identical terms, must be handed across the counter in quantities of not less than 20, otherwise they are liable to letter postage.

Unpaid, or insufficiently prepaid letters, etc., are charged double rates.

On payment of ½d certificates of posting of all ordinary (unregistered) correspondence may be obtained.

FOREIGN MAILS.

Days of Despatch and Rates of Postage from Perth—Uncertain.

*British Colonies and U.S.A.—2d for first ounce. Each ounce or part thereof, 1d, after first.

Other Countries—First ounce 2½d and 1½d for each succeeding ounce or part thereof.

PARCEL POST.

Parcels are received at any Post Office in the United Kingdom for transmission by Inland and Foreign and Colonial Parcel Post. The inland rates are:—not exceeding 2 lbs. 9d.; 2 lbs. to 5 lbs. 1/-; 5 lbs. to 8 lbs. 1/3; 8 lbs. to 11 lbs., 1/6. The maximum length allowed is 3 ft. 6 in., and length and girth combined is 6 ft. Glass, bottles, fish, game, meat, etc., if carefully packed and protected, may be transmitted, but on no account must bladders containing liquid, live animals, gunpowder, lucifer matches, or anything liable to sudden combustion, be sent by this conveyance. Parcels must not be posted in a letter box, but must be handed across Post Office counter. Box closing slightly earlier than for letters. Every parcel must bear a clear address, and this should be on the cover. Certificates of posting may be obtained without charge, and parcels can be registered at the same rates as for letters. Foreign and Colonial Parcel Post information may be obtained at any Post Office.

TELEGRAPH.

Telegraph rates.—Messages are sent to any postal telegraph office in Great Britain or Ireland, at a charge of 1/- for the first 12 words, and 1d. for every additional word. An additional 6d. is charged for each telegram handed in on Sundays. Addresses of senders and receivers are charged for. Cablegrams are accepted to all parts of Europe, America, India, China, and Australia; Radiotelegrams are also accepted. Charges, etc., may be learned at the post office. Deferred-rate cablegrams liable to be deferred 24 hours and day Cable Letters are also accepted.

MODE OF DELIVERY AND CHARGES.

When the terminal office, *i.e.*, the office nearest to the address is a Head Post Office, the amount paid for transmission covers the cost of delivery within three miles or within the town postal delivery when that extends for more than three miles. But when it is not a Head Post Office, the message is delivered free within three miles only. When the address is beyond the free delivery, porterage is charged at the rate of 6d. per mile or part of a mile, the charge being calculated from the boundary of the free delivery.

Week days—Office open from 8 a.m. to 7 p.m.

Sundays—9 to 10 a.m.

C

TELEPHONES.

Rates for Telephone Rentals according to distance of Subscriber's residence or office from Exchange.

The fees for the use of the Trunk Lines are as follows:—

For 25 miles or under,	...	...	...	4d*
For 50 ,, ,,	...	...	...	8d*
For 75 ,, ,,	...	...	...	1/-*
For 100 ,, ,,	...	...	...	1/4*
For every additional 40 miles or fraction thereof,				8d*

the unit period being three minutes, but no longer period than six minutes is allowed for any call.

Between 7.0 p.m. and 7.0 a.m. a six minutes' call is charged for as a three minutes' call—day rates; and during the same period a three minutes' call—for which the day rate is 1/—is charged 8d, and half the usual day charge is made where the ordinary fee is 1/4 or more.

Foreign Telephones—For particulars see P.O. Guide, or apply at local Post Office.

*Subject to revisal at early date.

RAILWAYS.

CALEDONIAN RAILWAY.

J. Smyth, district traffic superintendent, Perth
E. G. Moon, district engineer, Perth

HIGHLAND RAILWAY.

W. H. Cox, Esq., chairman
Robert Park, general manager
Head Offices—Inverness

NORTH BRITISH RAILWAY.

Mr. M'Robbie, district superintendent for north district, including Perth.
P. Proven, general traffic agent, Perth.

PERTH GENERAL STATION JOINT COMMITTEE.

J. Hamilton Houldsworth, Director of Caledonian Company
A. B. Gilroy } Directors of North British
Charles Carlow } Company
Marquis of Breadalbane, K.G. } Directors of Highland
Albert E. Pullar } Company.
Engineer—E. G. Moon
Station Superintendent—J. Hardman.

RAILWAY CARRIERS.

Wordie & Co., Mill Street, receive and deliver goods and parcels for Caledonian, Highland, and Great North of Scotland Railway Company; J. & P. Cameron for North British Railway Company

THE PERTH BRANCH OF THE BRITISH MEDICAL ASSOCIATION

President—Dr. Ferguson Watson.
Honorary Secretary—Dr. J. Hume, Perth.
Honorary Treasurer—Dr. Parker Stewart.
Representative to Annual Meeting—Dr. Stewart.
Branch Council—Drs. Bisset, Menzies, and Trotter, Perth,
Dr. Edwards, Bridge of Earn, Dr. Burgess, Stanley,

BANKS.

HOURS OF PUBLIC BUSINESS—From 10 to 3 o'clock every lawful day, except Saturday, when the Banks shut at Twelve noon.

STATUTORY HOLIDAYS—New Year's Day, Christmas Day (if either fall on a Sunday, the following Monday is kept), and Good Friday, First Monday in May, First Monday in August

LOCAL HOLIDAYS—Open 9 to 11 a.m.

BANK OF SCOTLAND, St. John Street.

Donald Mackenzie, agent

J. A. Cameron, accountant; T. C. Boyd, Thomas Donaldson, and Edward Strachan, tellers; A. MacPherson and R. G. Williamson, check clerks

W. Donaldson, messenger

WEST END BRANCH—35 South Methven Street

Jas. Young, agent | William Renfrew, teller

Branches.	Agents.	Branches.	Agents.
Aberfeldy	D. Macdiarmid	Co.-Angus	Wm. Irvine
Auchterarder	James S. Leslie	Crieff	Robert Allan
Blackford	D. S. Stewart	Dunblane	J. Barty
Blairgowrie	A.W.Henderson	Dunkeld	Thos. A. Peacock
Callander	R. S. Potts	Killin	Ewen MacEwan
		Pitlochry	John Fergusson

Draw on London Office, Bishopsgate, E.C.; the Bank of England, &c., &c.

ROYAL BANK OF SCOTLAND, 197 High Street.

R. B. Langwill, agent

A. G. MacCallum, accountant

London—Draw on Messrs. Coutts & Co.; Bank of England and London Office; Bank of Ireland and branches

Branches.	Agents.	Branches.	Agents.
Alyth	John Yeaman	Meigle	Rob. Shepherd
Blairgowrie	David Mitchell and Fred Will		

BRITISH LINEN BANK—77 George Street

John Stewart, P. R. Bulk, W.S., and
David Mackenzie, W.S., agents.
David Thomson, accountant

WEST END BRANCH—Caledonian Road
James Shankland, agent

CRIEFF BRANCH.—James Robertson, agent.
Draw on London Office, 41 Lombard Street; the Bank of England; and Smith, Payne, & Smiths

---

COMMERCIAL BANK OF SCOTLAND (Limited), 36 South Street.

Walter Mitchell, agent

J. J. Russell, accountant; J. W. Boyd, teller

Branches.	Agents.	Branches.	Agents.
Aberfeldy	Alex. Macdonald & Jas. Meikle	Comrie	John A. Mason
Abernethy	Thos. W. Faichney	Crieff	Alex. T. Halliburton
Blairgowrie	A. W. Bennett	Newburgh	Thos. W. Faichney
Callander	M'Michael & Buchanan	Pitlochry	D. Ross Mackay

Draw on London Office—62 Lombard Street

NATIONAL BANK OF SCOTLAND (Limited), 9 High Street

J. G. Farquharson, agent; John MacKenzie, accountant
A. P. Powrie, teller.

WEST END BRANCH, South Methven Street
J. G. Farquharson and Wm. Walker, joint agents
T. W. Reid, teller.
Draw on London Office, 37 Nicholas Lane, E.C.

UNION BANK OF SCOTLAND (Limited), 24 George Street.

Lewis Gibson, agent

D. G. Dickie, accountant

W.A. Raffan, } tellers
G. R. Goodlad, }

Draw on London Office, 62 Cornhill, E.C.; the Bank of England, and Messrs. Coutts & Co.

Branches.	Agents.	Branches.	Agents.
Aberfeldy......Chas. Munro &		Dunblane ......Chas. Chick	
W. Munro, joint-agents		Dunkeld.........R. M'Gillewie	
Auchterarder., Thos. E. Young		Dunning........W. Brown	
Blair-Atholl...J. R. Mackenzie		Errol............Wm. Goodall	
sub-agent		Killin............P. M'Neil	
Blairgowrie...W. H. Cromarty		Kincardine....Thos. Hardie	
Co.-Angus .....James Bell		Pitlochry.....Hugh Mitchell, B.	
Crieff.....John Dinwoodie		W. Liddell and A. M.	
		Meldrum, joint agents.	

THE CLYDESDALE BANK (Limited), 3 St. John Street.

John A. Stewart and Campbell, agents.
George Dickie, sub-agent.

Draw on London Office, 30 Lombard Street, E.C.3

Crieff—Charles R. Fleming, agent

Affiliated with and draw on all Branches of the London Joint City and Midland Bank, Ltd.

NORTH OF SCOTLAND AND TOWN AND COUNTY BANK (Limited
13 Scott Street,

Alex. Duff and Robert Hunter, agents.
James D. Petrie, accountant
Branch Office at Hay's Mart.

S. Methven Street

James Robertson and Thomas Dempster, agents
Andrew M. Mechie, accountant

Alyth—A. M. Ferguson, agent

Draw on National Provincial and Union Bank of England, Ltd., 2 Princes Street, London, E.C. 2, Messrs. Barclay & Co. (Limited), Bankers, London, and London Joint City and Midland Bank (Limited), London.

THE SAVINGS BANK OF THE COUNTY AND CITY OF PERTH, CERTIFIED UNDER THE ACT OF 1863
(*Founded 1815*).

W. A. Barclay, actuary and cashier; John Petrie, accountant; James Jackson, branch supervisor; J. & R. Morison & Co., C.A., auditors; Lewis Gibson, Esq., treasurer

The Head Office, 26 Tay Street, and West End Branch, 39 County Place, Perth, are open every day from 10 till 3 o'clock, except Saturday, when they close at 12

Open on Saturday evening from 6 to 8 o'clock for receiving deposits ONLY

BRANCHES—COUNTY

ABERFELDY—James Morgan, cashier

ALYTH—A. M. Ferguson, North of Scotland and Town and County Bank, Ltd., cashier

AUCHTERARDER—J. P. Kennaway, solicitor, cashier

BLAIRGOWRIE—William Craigie, cashier

CALLANDER—Donald M'Laren, solicitor, cashier

CAPUTH—Anna M. Miller, cashier

COUPAR-ANGUS—David Culross, cashier

CRIEFF—John Dinwoodie, Union Bank of Scotland, Limited cashier

DUNBLANE—John Stewart, solicitor, cashier

DUNKELD—Archibald Buchanan, cashier

DUNNING—William Brown, Union Bank of Scotland, Limited, cashier

PITLOCHRY—Hugh Mitchell, Solicitor, cashier

SOCIETY OF SOLICITORS.

This Society was instituted in 1825, and is now incorporated by Royal Charter, dated 14th February, 1857, into a body politic and corporate, by the name of "The Society of Procurators and Solicitors in the City and County of Perth." The main object of the Society was the Establishment of a Law Library; and accordingly, there has been formed an extensive collection of books, containing almost every work immediately relating to the profession. There is a standing committee of management appointed annually, consisting of the office-bearers and five members.

OFFICE-BEARERS--President, J. Lyall Bowie; Vice-President Thos. Macpherson; Secretary, A. C. Campbell; Treasurer, James Mitchell; Librarian, J. Ritchie.

COMMITTEE OF MANAGEMENT--Office-Bearers, George Purves, Thomas Dempster, P. H. Macfarlane, J. T. Douglas, and T. B. Marshall.

AUDITORS--J. W. Wyllie and D. M. Mackay.

Sub-Librarian--Sergeant Murray.

MEMBERS.

Anderson, Walter, Perth	1919	Macfarlane, P.H.,A'ter'der	1912
Bates, R. Martin, Perth	1911	Mackay, David M., Perth	1918
Begg, John, Perth	1899	Mackay, Donald, Perth	1919
Bowie, J. Lyall, Perth	1894	Mackenzie, David, Perth	1909
Boyd, Chas., Co.-Angus	1896	Macnab, Duncan, Perth	1901
Black, R. R., Blairgowrie	1907	Macpherson, Thos., Perth	1894
Buik, P. R., Perth	1917	Marshall, David, Perth	1901
Cameron, John C., Perth	1919	Marshall, T. B., Perth	1915
Campbell, A. C., Perth	1908	Miller, Andrew, Perth	1901
Campbell, Chas. P., Perth	1917	Miller, George A., do.	1896
Campbell, John, Perth	1911	Miller, Jn. B., Bl'gowrie	1870
Campbell, Robert, Perth	1908	Miller, John G., Perth	1896
Clow, Andrew, Aberfeldy	1919	Mitchell, Hugh, Pitlochry	1890
Dempster, Thomas, Perth	1900	Mitchell, James, Perth	1897
Douglas, J. T., Perth	1913	Mitchell, J. W. Rollo, P'th	1903
Drysdale, S., Crieff	1893	Munro, C. J. D., Aberfeldy	1919
Ferguson, A. M., Alyth	1907	Munro, Wm., Perth	1909
Finlayson, M., Crieff	1887	Purves, George, Perth	1910
Forrest, A. G., Perth	1906	Ritchie, John, Perth	1892
Gordon, C. H., Perth	1902	Robertson, James, Perth	1888
Gray, G. N., Perth	1900	Ross, C. D. M., Crieff	1907
Hunter, Robert, Perth	1898	Sneddon, A. M., Perth	1901
Keay, Wm., Blairgowrie	1907	Stewart, Alexander, Perth	1903
Kennaway, J.P., A'ter'der	1917	Stewart, Robert, do.	1904
Kippen, R. M., Perth	1891	Strang, Peter, do.	1903
Little, John, Perth	1914	Thomas, J H., do.	1891
Logan, Thos., Perth	1899	Wyllie, J. W., Perth	1902
MacBeth, J., A'terarder	1893	Yeaman, John, Alyth	1898
Macbeth, Alex., Pitlochry	1907	Young, W. Cochrane, P'th	1875

The Library of the Society is in the County Buildings, and is open from 10 A.M. to 4 P.M. Saturday, 10 to 1.

WARDS FOR ELECTION OF TOWN COUNCIL.

FIRST WARD.

Commencing by a line drawn from the centre of the River Tay westwards, to and along the centre of Victoria Street, to and northwards along the centre of King Street and South Methven Street to High Street Port; thence eastwards along the centre of High Street to the centre of the River Tay, and thence along the centre of that river to the point of commencement.

Polling Place—Central District School.

SECOND WARD.

Commencing by a line drawn from the centre of High Street Port to and along the centre of South Methven Street and King Street, to and eastwards along the centre of Victoria Street to the centre of the Willowgate Branch of the River Tay; thence southwards along the centre of the said Willowgate branch to the south-east corner of Moncreiffe Island, thence westwards to and along the centre of the River Tay to and around. the eastern and southern boundaries of Friarton Farm, thence northwards to and along the north-east side of the Edinburgh Road to the mouth of Moncreiffe Tunnel of the Caledonian Railway, thence north-westwards along that railway to the General Railway Station, thence northwards to and along the centre of Caledonian Road to the centre of West High Street, thence eastwards along the centre o f that street to the point of commencement.

Polling Place—Caledonian Road School.

THIRD WARD.

Commencing by a line drawn from the centre of the junction of York Place with Caledonian Road, to and southwards along the centre of Caledonian Road to the General Railway Station, thence along the Caledonian Railway to the mouth of Moncreiffe Tunnel, thence northwestwards to the existing Burgh boundary at the cistern on St. Magdalen's Farm, thence along that boundary to the Glasgow Road at Cherrybank, thence westwards along the centre of the Scouring or Craigie Burn, to and northwards along the west side of the road on the west side of the Fever Hospital, to and thence eastwards along the centre of the road on the north side of said Hospital to Gowrie Bank, thence in a straight line to the centre of the Glasgow Road at the south end of Rose-crescent, thence along the centre of the Glasgow Road to the point of commencement.

Polling Place—Craigie School.

FOURTH WARD.

Commencing by a line drawn from the centre of High Street Port westwards to and along the centre of West High Street, to and along the centre of Caledonian Road, to and along the centre of York Place and Glasgow Road to Rose Crescent; thence in a straight line westwards to and along the centre of the road on the north side of the Burghmuir Fever Hospital to the west side of the road on the west side of the said Hospital, thence northwards along the west side of the last-named road to Old Gallows Road, thence northwards across the fields to and eastwards along the centre of Crieff Road to the centre of the Town's Lade, thence southwards along the centre of the Town's Lade to the Military Barracks, thence along the north boundary of the Military Barracks, to and along the centre of Barrack Street, Atholl Street, and North and South Methven Streets, to the point of commencement.

Polling Place—Victoria Institute, Dovecotland.

FIFTH WARD.

Commencing by a line drawn from the centre of High Street Port, to and northwards along the centre of South and North Methven Streets, Atholl Street, and Barrack Street, to and along the north side of the Military Barracks, to and along the centre of the Town's Lade, to and westwards along the centre of Crieff Road to East Newton Lodge at Hillyland; thence along the west side of the schoolhouse there, and of the Newton Burn and Town's Lade to Tulloch Works; thence eastwards along the north side of the road leading to the Dunkeld Road at Muirton Toll, to and along the north side of the road leading from that Toll to South Muirton Farm, to and thence along the top of the North Inch, and thence southwards to and along the centre of the River Tay to a point opposite the centre of the foot of High Street, thence westwards to and along the centre of High Street to the point of commencement.

Polling Place—Perth Academy.

SIXTH WARD.

To embrace the whole of the Burgh of Perth as extended by the Perth Corporation Order, 1908, so far as situate on the east side of the centre of the River Tay above Moncreiffe Island and the centre of the Willowgate branch of that river.

Polling Place—Kinnoull School.

LORD PROVOSTS OF PERTH FROM 1639.

1639-49	Robert Arnott		1702-3	Patrick Davidson
50-51	Andrew Grant		4-5	Alexander Robertson
52	Andrew Buttar		6-7	James Cree
53-54	Robert Arnott		8-9	James Brown
55-58	Andrew Buttar		10-11	William Austin
59-60	John Paterson		12-13	Robt. Robertson, jun.
61	Andrew Grant		14	William Austin
62-63	Andrew Buttar		15	Pat. Hay, appointed by the Earl of Mar, for the Pretender
64-69	Patrick Thriepland			
70	George Thriepland			
71-73	Patrick Thriepland		16-17	Robt. Robertson, jun.
74	Sir Patrick Thriepland		18-19	William Austin
75	Archibald Chrystie		20-21	Robert Robertson
76			22-23	William Austin
77-78	Patrick Hay		24-25	William Ferguson
79	Robert Lundie		26-27	Robert Robertson
80-81	John Glass		28-29	Colin Brown
82-83	Patrick Hay		30-31	Robert Robertson
84-86	John Glass		32-33	Patrick Crie
87	Sir Patrick Thriepland		34	Robert Robertson
88-90	Robert Smyth		35-36	Patrick Crie
91	George Oliphant		37-38	Robert Robertson
92-93	James Cree		39-40	James Crie
94-95	David Murray		41-42	Patrick Crie
96-97	James Cree		43-44	James Crie
98-99	Patrick Davidson		45	No election, owing to the Rebellion
1700-1	George Oliphant			

1746 Patrick Crie	1814-15 Robert Ross
47 Robert Robertson	16-17 Laurence Robertson
48-49 James Crie	18-19 David Morison
50-51 John Robertson	20-21 Robert Ross
52-53 James Crie	22-23 Pat. Gilbert Stewart
54-55 John Robertson	24-25 Robert Ross
56-57 James Crie	25-26 Pat. Gilbert Stewart
58-59 William Stuart	27-28 Robert Ross
60 William Gray	29-30 Patrick G. Stewart
61 William Stuart	31-32 John Wright
62-63 John Stuart	33-35 Adam Pringle
64-65 Alexander Simson	36-38 Robert Matthew
66-67 William Stuart	39-41 David Greig
68-69 John Stuart	42-46 Charles G. Sidey
70-71 Alexander Simson	47-49 David Clunie
72-73 William Stuart	50-55 James Dewar
74-75 Alexander Simson	56-61 William Imrie
76-77 William Stuart	62-64 Sir David Ross
78-79 George Fechney	65-67 Robert Kemp
80-81 William Stuart	68-73 John Pullar
82-83 George Fechney	73-74 Andrew Graham
84-85 Thomas Marshall	75-77 Archibald M'Donald
86-87 William Alison	78-80 Thomas Richardson
88-89 John Caw	80-82 Kirkwood Hewat
90-91 Alexander Fechney	83 John M'Leish
92-93 John Caw	84-87 Andrew Martin
94-95 James Ramsay	87-90 James Peter Whittet
96-97 Alexander Fechney	90-93 George Wilson
98-99 Thomas Black	93-99 Sir John A. Dewar, Bart.
1800-1 Thomas Hay Marshall	99-02 David Macgregor
2-3 John Caw	1902-5 Thomas Love
4-5 Thomas Hay Marshall	05-9 James Cuthbert
6-7 John Caw	09-12 Duncan Macnab
8-9 Laurence Robertson	12-19 Charles Scott
10-11 Robert Ross	19-21 A. Ure Wotherspoon
12-13 Laurence Robertson	

MAGISTRATES AND TOWN COUNCIL.

Arch. Ure Wotherspoon, Lord Provost
Alexander Frazer, Dean of Guild
1. David Cunningham.
2. Robert Campbell.   } Bailies
3. Alex. Gowans.
4. Jas. Simpson.

Hon. John Dewar, Treasurer

COUNCILLORS.

First Ward.

1920 H. Christie	1919 James Taylor
1920 James M'Cracken	1919 John Traill
1919 Robert Stewart	

Second Ward.

1919 J. L. Bowie	1919 John Downie
1920 James Currie	1919 Alex. Gowans

Third Ward.

1919 J. Dewar	1920 Thos. Macpherson
1919 Thomas Hunter	1919 James Simpson

Fourth Ward.

1919 A. W. Fisher	1919 R. M. Ross
1920 Wm. Paton	1920 James Stewart

Fifth Ward.

1920 David Cunningham	1920 Wm. Munro
1914 Nickel Crombie	1919 Robert Stewart

Sixth Ward.

1919 James Calderwood	1920 Wm. J. Wood
1919 A. U. Wotherspoon	1919 Robert Campbell

CITY CLERK—John Begg
DEPUTE CITY CLERK—James Turpie
CITY CHAMBERLAIN—Robert Keay, 1 High Street
BURGH ASSESSOR—Donald Mackintosh, Tay Street
BURGH SURVEYOR—Robert M'Killop
CHIEF CONSTABLE—John Scott
DEPUTE CHIEF CONSTABLE—W. Carstairs
BURGH PROSECUTOR—W. A. Boyes
SANITARY INSPECTOR—Wm. Asher

INCORPORATED TRADES
CONVENER COURT

Geo. P. K. Young, Deacon of Hammermen, *Convener*		
James M'Cash,	do	Bakers
W. Blair,	do	Glovers
Thomas Clark,	do	Wrights
Jas. C. Cairncross,	do	Tailors
Alexander Fenton,	do	Fleshers
John K. Norwell,	do	Shoemakers
James C. Smail,	do	Weavers

Robert Hunter, solicitor, clerk and treasurer

GUILDRY INCORPORATION OF PERTH AND GUILD COURT.

COMMITTEE OF MANAGEMENT.
Alexr. Frazer, Lord Dean of Guild.

Mr. W. F. D. Wallace	Mr. John M'Arthur
Mr. Geo. Stobie	Mr. Peter Thomson
Mr. Jas. M'Laren	Mr. George Henderson
Mr. Johnstone Edwards	Mr. Daniel M'Kenzie

GUILD COURT.
The Lord Dean of Guild.

The Lord Provost	Bailie Campbell
Bailie Cunningham	Bailie Gowans

MERCHANT COUNCILLORS.

Mr. George Bayne
Mr. Geo. Valentine

Mr. W. A. Barclay
Mr. Buchanan Dunsmore

TRADES COUNCILLORS.

Convener—Jas. M'Cash
Deacon—Thomas Clark

MEAL SEARCHERS.

Mr. J. B. M'Donald
Mr. David Barlas
Mr. Alex. Macgregor

Mr. J. Matthews
Mr. R. Drummond
Mr. D. Robertson

J. W. Rollo Mitchell, clerk and treasurer; Hugh Martin, land
steward ; William Spence, officer.

PARISH COUNCIL

Chairman of Council—David Ferrier
Chairman of Landward Committee—D. Mackenzie
Convener of Law and Finance Committee—D. Mackenzie
Convener of Review Committee—Peter Taylor
Convener of Poorhouse Committee—J. K. Tayor
Convener of Works Committee—John Thomson

Messrs Harry Christie
Peter Taylor
Robert Inglis
Rev. Father M'Daniel
David Ferrier
David Loudon
David Bruce
J. K. Taylor
Wm. Loney
James Macpherson

Messrs S. R. Aitken
James Beveridge
Alexr. Crow
Nickel Crombie
Ed. J. Glass
Peter Leitham
William Robertso
John Thomson
D. Mackenzie

OFFICIALS

Robert Stewart, inspector of poor and clerk to council
Jas. Duncan, assistant inspector
Annie C. Stewart, nurse assistant
John M. Bruce, clerk
John Clark, collector of poor rates
Walter F. Henderson, assistant collector
John R. Hutcheon, governor of poorhouse
Elizabeth M. C. Bennett, matron of do
James Davidson, gatekeeper of   do
Robert Stewart, secretary and treasurer of poorhouse
James Morison, auditor

PERTH HUNT, AS AT DECEMBER, 1920.

Right Hon. Lord Rollo, Preses ; Charles P. Campbell, solicitor, 61 George Street, secretary and treasurer.

MEMBERS.

His Grace, The Duke of Atholl, K.T., C.B., M.V.O., D.S.O., Blair Castle, Blair Atholl

Frederick Black, Esq., of Balgowan, Balgowan, Perth

The Most Hon. The Marquis of Breadalbane, K.G., Taymouth Castle, Aberfeldy

Capt. E. M. Murray Buchanan, of Leny, Leny, Callander

G. A. Buchanan, Esq. of Gask, Gask, Auchterarder

Major Ian Bullough, M.C., of Meggernie, Lochs, Glenlyon

Colonel Charles A. J. Butter, of Pitlochry, Pitlochry

David Rutherford Lindsay Carnegie, Esq., of Ashintully, Ashintully, Blairgowrie

Geo. Clark, Esq., of Straloch, Straloch, Kirkmichael

W. H. Coats, Esq., of Bertha, Battleby House, Perth

Sir Stuart Coats, Bart., M.C., of Ballathie, Ballathie, Stanley

Captain James S. Coats, M.C., Ballathie, Stanley

A. E. Cox, Esq. of Dungarthill, Dungarthill, Dunkeld

Ronald Cox, Esq., Yr. of Dungarthill, Dungarthill, Dunkeld

W. H. Cox, of Snaigow, Snaigow, Murthly

Alfred W. Cox, Esq. of Glendoick, Glendoick, Glencarse

Euan Cox, Esq., Yr. of Glendoick, Glendoick, Glencarse

Colonel Alexander H. O. Dennistoun, of Golfhill

Major The Hon. John Dewar, Luncarty

W. Arthur Dewhurst, Esq., of Summerhill, Summerhill, Stanley

A. Gregor Dixon, Esq., of Glentulchan, Glentulchan, Glenalmond

Capt. Malcolm Drummond, of Megginch, Megginch Castle, Errol

Colonel Arthur Hay Drummond, of Cromlix, Cromlix, Dunblane

Sir W. C. Dunbar, Bart., of Mochrum, Earnbank, Bridge of Earn

The Right Hon. The Lord Dunedin, of Stenton, Stenton, Dunkeld

The Right Hon. Lord Forteviot, of Dupplin, Dupplin Castle, Perth

The Right Hon. Lord Faringdon, of Glenalmond, Glenalmond House, Perth

Charles Drummond Forbes, of Millearne, Millearne, Auchterarder

Major Fred Foster, of Faskally Faskally, Pitlochry

Colonel W. T. J. S. Steuart Fothringham, of Fothringham and Murthly, Murthly Castle, Murthly

Colonel A. M. B. Graham, T.D., of Gleny, Arntomy, Port of Menteith

Anthony G. Maxtone Graham, Esq., of Cultoquhey and Redgorton, Redgorton, Perth

Andrew J. G. Murray Graham, Esq., of Murrayshall, 23 Rutland Gate, S.W.

J. G. Hay Halkett, Esq., of Balendoch, Balendoch, Meigle

Colonel J. A. Richardson Drummond Hay, of Seggieden, Seggieden, Perth

R. Wylie Hill, Esq., of Balthayock, Balthayock, Perth

Major The Hon. Hermon-Hodge, Luncarty

Walter Jones, Esq., Aberuchit, Castle. Crieff

Charles Y. Kinloch, Esq., Vancouver

Sir George Kinloch, Bart., of Kinloch, O.B.E., Kinloch, Blairgowrie

Capt. David Lumsden, M.C., Huntingtowerfield, Perth

Alex. P. Lyle, Esq., of Glendelvine, Glendelvine, Murthly

Major Arch. M. P. Lyle, Esq., M.C., Yr., of Glendelvine, Powis House, Stirling

W. G. M'Beth, Esq. of Dunira, Dunira, Comrie

David M'Cowan, Esq., Monzie Castle, Crieff

Robert Finnie M'Ewan, Esq., of Bardrochat, Bardrochat, Colmonell, Ayrshire

Commodore Sir Malcolm Macgregor, Bart., R.N., C.B., C.M.G., of Macgregor, Edinchip, Balquhidder, R.S.O.

Alexander R. MacGregor, Esq., The Broich, Crieff

Sir Kenneth J. Mackenzie, Bart., of Gairloch, 10 Moray Place, Edinburgh

R. W. R. Mackenzie, Esq., of Earlshall, Earlshall, Leuchars, Fife

William C. Macpherson, Esq., C.S.I., of Blairgowrie, Blairgowrie House, Blairgowrie

The Right Hon. The Earl of Mansfield, Scone Palace, Perth

Willliam D. Graham Menzies, Esq., of Hallyburton, Hallyburton, Coupar-Angus

Major William F. Middleton, of Baldarroch, Baldarroch, Murthly

John Middleton, Esq., Yr, of Baldarroch, Baldarroch. Murthly

Wm. S. Miller, Esq. of Balmanno, Balmanno Castle, Bridge of Earn

Col Sir R. D. Moncreiffe, Bart., C.M.G. and D.A.T., of Moncreiffe, Moncrieffe House, Bridge of Earn

Commander Guy Moncrieffe, R.N., Moncrieffe House, Bridge of Earn

Sir Ernest R. Moon, K.C.B., K.C., Balhomie, Cargill

Captain W. A. Home Drummond Moray, of Abercairny, Abercairny, Perth

The Right Hon. The Earl of Moray, Kinfauns Castle, Perth

Sir A. K. Muir, Bart., of Blairdrummond, Deanston, Doune

Jas. F. Muir, Esq. of Braco, Braco Castle, Braco

Sir Torquill Munro, Bart., of Lindertis, Lindertis, Kirriemuir

Major The Hon. A. D. Murray, of Pitfour, Pitfour Castle, Perth

Chas. A. Murray, Esq., Taymount, Stanley

Archibald J. P. Murray, Esq., Logie House, Methven

The Hon. Ronald Graham Murray, Stenton, Dunkeld

The Rt. Hon. Lord James T. Stewart Murray, Blair Castle Blair-Atholl

N. J. Nasmyth, Esq., of Glen Farg, Glen Farg House

Sir Herbert K. Oglilvy, Bart., o' Inverquharity, Baldovan House, Dundee

The Right Hon. The Earl of Perth

Captain J. Douglas Ramsay, yr., of Bamff, Estates Office, Balmoral Castle, Ballater

Col. P. R. Burn Clerk-Rattray, of Craighall, Craighall, Rattray, Blairgowrie

Major Neil Stewart Richardson, D.S.O., Seggieden

Gordon Richmond, Esq., Meigle House, Meigle

Jas. Richmond, Esq., Kippenross, Dunblane

Major James Stewart Robertson, of Edradynate, Edradynate, Strathtay

Ernest F. Robertson, Esq., of Auchleeks, Craigenveoch, Aberfoyle

Capt. N. F. W. Rockey of Lawers, Lawers, Comrie

James A. Rollo, Esq., County Club, Perth

The Right Hon. Lord Rollo, Duncrub, Dunning

The Right Hon. The Lord Ruthven of Gowrie, Carlton Club, S.W. 1

Alastair C. Sandeman, Esq., of Fonab, Fonab, Pitlochry

The Rt. Hon. The Lord Sempill, Fintray, Aberdeenshire

The Right Hon. Lord Scone, Scone Palace, Perth

Col. David M. Smythe, of Methven, Moulin Almond, Perth

Major Alexander Blair Stewart, of Balnakeilly, Balnakeilly, Pitlochry

Brig.-General Arch. Stirling, of Keir, Keir, Dunblane

Major Carolus H. Graham Stirling of Strowan, Seafield, Comrie

John Stroyan, Esq., of Lanrick, Lanrick Castle, Doune

Capt. O. A. Taylor, of Ballendrick, Ballendrick, Bridge of Earn

Captain F. de Sales la Terriere, Dunalastair, Rannoch

Græme A. Whitelaw, Esq., 1 Lowther Gardens, Prince's Gate, S.W.

Lt.-Col. T. E. L. Hill Whitson, 14th Hussars, of Parkhill, Cavalry Club, Piccadilly, London

J. Moncrieff Wright, Esq., Kinmonth, Bridge of Earn

Major D. Moncrieff Wright, Kinmonth, Bridge of Earn

SPORTING CLUBS, &c.

PERTH BOWLING CLUB (Green, Balhousie).
Dr. Parker Stewart, president; H. Thomson, ex-president; A. Bain, hon. secretary; Neil Gow, hon. treasurer.

KINNOULL BOWLING CLUB (Green, Muirhall Terrace).
J. R. Fenwick, president; A. M. Mechie, hon. treasurer; — Adams, hon. secretary.

WEST END BOWLING CLUB (Green, Glover Street, Craigie).
Jas. Shankland, president; R. M'Leod vice-president; Jas. Finlayson, treasurer; R. C. Docherty, secretary.

CALEDONIAN BOWLING CLUB (Green, Feus Road).
W. Fraser, president; W. Loney, vice-president; James Murdoch, hon. secretary; John Lamond, hon. treasurer.

PERTH LAWN TENNIS CLUB.
Secretary and treas., W. Mowat Wilson, 10 Princes Street.

THE NEW WHIST CLUB, TAY STREET.
President—J. J. Donald; Committee—George Brady, ex-Provost M'Nab, Andrew Butters, Alex. Frazer, Robert Campbell, James J. Donald, John K. Norwell, R. Hay Robertson, David Thomson; sec., D. Thomson; treas., H. Meldrum.

PERTH COUNTY CRICKET CLUB, LIMITED.
President, A K Bell, Esq.; captain, W. Lovat Fraser; hon. secretary, A. Latto; hon. treasurer, Neil Gow, St. John Street.

ROYAL PERTH GOLFING SOCIETY AND COUNTY AND CITY CLUB.—
R. W. R. Mackenzie, Esq., captain. H. J. Bell, hon. secretary and treasurer. J. Moncrieff Wright, Esq., P. R. Buik, Esq., J. G. Miller, Esq., Walter Mitchell, Esq., Sir G. Kinloch, Bart., J. Stewart Robertson, Esq., A. E. Pullar, Esq., Earl of Mansfield, A. G. Heiton, Esq., Capt. O. A. Taylor, councillors.

KING JAMES the SIXTH GOLF CLUB.—P. W. Campbell, captain; Capt Lowe, secretary.

CRAIGIE HILL GOLF CLUB, LTD.—A. J. Cameron, captain; John Campbell, solicitor, 5 St. John Street, secretary.

PERTH ANGLER'S CLUB (Instituted 1858).—Patron, The Right Hon. the Earl of Mansfield. President, Kenneth Annandale. Secretary and treasurer, P. D. Malloch, Scott Street.

PERTHSHIRE FISHING CLUB (Instituted 1880).—President, A. J. Cameron. Hon. secretary and treasurer, J. Malloch, Scott Street.

PERTH CITY AND COUNTY MINIATURE RIFLE CLUB (affiliated to the Society of Miniature Rifle Clubs)—President, Major Herbert S. Pullar. Hon. Secretary and Hon. treasurer, J. Shankland, British Linen Bank (West End Branch), Perth.

PERTHSHIRE RIFLE ASSOCIATION.—Chairman—Major Herbert S. Pullar, Scottish Horse. Hon. Sec. & Treas.—Capt. John Little, 10 Blackfriars St , Perth.

PERTHSHIRE NATURAL HISTORY MUSEUM, Tay St.

Open daily from 9.30 a.m. to 5 p.m., except Tuesdays, from 9.30 till 1.

Chairman of Committee—Councillor Jas. Stewart.
Curator—John Ritchie, jun.

PERTHSHIRE SOCIETY OF NATURAL SCIENCE.

Established in 1867 to promote the study of Natural Science, and to elucidate the Natural History of Perthshire. The Society meets in the Lecture Hall in the Perthshire Natural History Museum, Tay Street, on the 2nd Friday of every month from November to May, and in the other months has excursions to various parts of Perthshire. The annual meeting is held on the 2nd Friday of March, when the Council and other officers for the succeeding year are appointed. The membership of the Society is about 400.

COUNCIL.

President—Mr. G. F. Bates, B.A., B.Sc.

Vice-presidents—Mr. James Menzies, Mr. Edward Smart, B.A., B.Sc., Mr. W. T. Morrison, Mr. J. J. Simpson. Secretary—Mr. W. G. Mitchell, Tayview Bank, Craigie. Treasurer—Mr. James Winier, 35 George Street (A. Darling & Co.). Librarian—Mr. James Clacher. Editor—Mr. E. J. Balfour, M.A., B.Sc. Councillors—Mr. W. Barclay, Mr. R. H. Meldrum, Mr. T. M'Laren, Mr. J. Asher, Mr. S. T. Ellison. Curator Mr. John Ritchie, Jun.

BRIDGEND INSTITUTE.

President—Mr. W. Leslie Beaton; secy., Mr. Fred. J. Forbes, Isla, Perth; treasurer, Mr. Chas. Robertson.

Reading-room open daily from 10 a.m. to 9 p.m Library open Monday and Thursday evenings from 8 to 9 p.m. Subscription of membership, 2s 6d per annum; family ticket, 3s 6d; honorary membership, 10s 6d.

Hall available for meetings, dances, etc. For terms apply to the Secretary.

SANDEMAN PUBLIC LIBRARY.

Members of the Council—Lord Provost Wotherspoon; Treas. Dewar; ex-Bailies Calderwood and Crombie; Councillors Currie, Fisher, Munro, Wood, R. Stewart, and Traill; Householders—Ex-Lord Provost Macnab, ex-Dean of Guild Barlas, Messrs. William Barclay, James Nicol, John Ritchie, R. Hay Robertson, Dougald Walker, John C. Cameron, John S. Jarvie, Rev. P. R. Landreth. Clerk & Librarian —James Craigie. Chairman—Lord Provost Wotherspoon

PERTH CITY MISSION.

President—Wm. Ellison, J P.; Vice-president, D. Ferrier, Esq.; hon. secy., J. Lyall Bowie, Esq., solicitor; hon. treasurer, James Robertson, Esq.; missionaries, John W. Galletly, and Mrs. Todd,

ROYAL HORTICULTURAL SOCIETY OF PERTHSHIRE

INSTITUTED 1806.

Has meetings for competition in fruits, flowers, &c.

The King, patron.

F. Norie-Miller, Esq., president; A. W. Brown, Esq., and Wm. Barclay, Esq., vice-presidents; Mr. J. S. Campbell, practical vice-president; Mr. James Young, seedsman, 189 High Street, Perth, secy. and treas.

HIGH CONSTABLES.

Wm. Munro, moderator.

Dr. E. L. Paton, physician.
Rev. Walter E. Lee, chaplain.

Captains—1st Division, A. G. Chalmers; 2nd Division, Crichton; 3rd Division, D. A. Stewart; 4th Division, P. F. Macgregor; 5th Division, Alex. Stirling; 6th Division, J. Dow.

Secretary, Sinclair Grant, Craigie.

Treasurer, W. P. Macpherson, Pitcullen.

Custodier, Councillor Calderwood. Solicitor, G. N. Gray.

PERTH LANDLORDS' AND PROPERTY AGENTS' ASSOCIATION.

President, James Robertson, Solicitor; Secretary and Treasurer, John Little, Solicitor, 10 Blackfriars Street.

PERTH ROTARY CLUB.

Council—President, J. J. Forbes, M.Ph.S., 7 Scott Street; Immediate Past President, F. Norie-Miller, J.P., F.E.I.S.; Vice-President, F. Eastman, Kinnoull Street; Hon. Secy., Robert Campbell, solicitor; Hon. Treas., Alex. Duff, J.P., North of Scotland Bank, Scott Street; J. Mayhew Allen, Neil Gow, R. Halley, A. W. Fisher, W. A. Barclay, G. J. Mathews.

CHARITABLE INSTITUTIONS.

COUNTY AND CITY OF PERTH ROYAL INFIRMARY AND DISPENSARY.

Sir Robert D. Moncreiffe, Bart., chairman; The Hon. Archibald Ure Wotherspoon, Lord Provost of Perth, deputy chairman; John C. Cameron, solicitor, 2 Charlotte Street, Perth, secretary; James Robertson, solicitor, South Methven Street, treasurer; Messrs. J. & R. Morison & Co., C.A., auditors; R. Stirling, M.D., F.R.C.S.E., hon. consulting surgeon; W. Hope Fowler, M.B., Ch.B., F.R.C.S.E., hon. consulting medical electrician; J. J. Donald, hon. pharmacist; Mr. L. Turton Price, chief surgeon and gynæcologist; Alexander Trotter, M.B., Ch.B., J. B. Wilkie, M.B., Ch.B., F.R.C.S.E., surgeons; E. L. Paton, M.B., C.M., J. Edwards, M.B., Ch.B., W. Fraser Bisset, M.B., Ch.B., D.P.H., physicians; John Hume, M.B., C.M., D.P.H., out-patient medical officer; James Edwards, M.B., Ch.B., clinical pathologist; W. Fraser Bisset, M.B., Ch.B., D.P.H., medical electrician; Alexander Trotter, M.B., Ch.B.; oculist and aurist; W. L. Hunter, M.B., Ch.B., and H. Mackinnon, M.B., Ch.B., house surgeons; Miss Bessie D. Bowhill, Matron.

PERTHSHIRE BIBLE SOCIETY.

President, Sheriff Sym; Vice-President, Mr J. L. Bowie, Treasurer, R. S. Niven; Secretary,

INDIGENT OLD MEN'S SOCIETY.

Patron—Right Hon. Lord Kinnaird.

Mr. R. M. Kippen, president; ex-Bailie Taylor, Mr. Jas. A. Peebles, ex-Dean of Guild Chalmers, Mr. James E. Fenwick, vice-presidents; Mr. Peter Fleming, 212 High Street, secretary; Mr. J. Lyall Bowie, treasurer.

SCOTCH GIRLS' FRIENDLY SOCIETY.

PERTH BRANCHES I. and II.
President—(acting) Mrs. Macgregor, of St. Leonard's Bank.
Hon. Treasurer—Miss Stirling.
Hon. Secretary—Mrs. Fisher, Boatlands.
Lady Superintendent—Miss Emslie.
Lodge—72 South Tay Street.

PERTH SICK POOR NURSING SOCIETY.

Chairman, John Ritchie, Esq.; President of Ladies' Committee, Lady Georgina Home Drummond; Secretary and Treasurer; Chas. P. Campbell, solicitor; Nurses, Miss M'Calman, Miss Ross, and Miss Young.

Scones Lethendy Mortifications.

The Ministers and Elders of the Burgh of Perth, trustees; the Lord Provost, Bailies, and Ministers of the Burgh, patrons, Andrew Miller, solicitor, clerk; James Mackie, treasurer; M. Duigan, officer.

King James Sixth's Hospital.

The Ministers and Elders of the Burgh of Perth, managers; James Mackie, Hospital master; Andrew Miller, solicitor, clerk.

Eleemosynaries must continue to reside within the ancient boundaries of the burgh of Perth as long as they enjoy the appointments, and in the event of their leaving the said boundaries they will be struck off the roll.

Perth Ladies' House of Refuge for Destitute Girls (Industrial School), Craigie.

The Right Hon. the Marchioness of Breadalbane, Lady Moncreiffe, Lady Georgina Home Drummond, and Mrs. Richmond of Kincairney, patronesses.

The Right Hon. Anna, Countess of Moray, president; Mrs. Bannerman, Abernyte, Inchture, Mrs. Crawford, Orchil, Mrs. Moncrieff Wright, Kinmonth, Mrs. A. E. Pullar, Durn, Mrs. H. S. Pullar, Dunbarney Cottage, and Mrs. Coats, Battleby, vice-presidents; Dr. F. O. Moffat, physician; Mrs. M'Cash and David Mackenzie, W.S., secys.; J. & R. Morison & Co., C.A., auditors; Condie, Mackenzie, & Co., treas.; Miss Kelman, matron

Perth Girls' School of Industry, Wellshill.

The Most Honourable the Marchioness of Breadalbane, The Right Hon. the Countess of Moray, The Right Hon. the Countess of Kinnoull, The Right Hon. the Countess-Dowager of Dudley, Lady Muir Mackenzie, Miss Drummond, Mains of Megginch, Lady Forteviot of Dupplin Castle, Miss Smythe of Methven, patronesses.

The Right Hon. The Countess of Mansfield, hon. president; Hon. Mrs. Smythe of Methven, president; Mrs. Albert Butter, Duntanlich; Mrs. Macduff, Bonhard; Mrs. Black, Keillour Castle; Mrs. Fraser, Invermay, vice-presidents; Mrs. Geo. Miller, Knowehead, hon. sec.; P. Nisbet, C.A., 5 St. John Street, hon. treas. Dr. Moffat, hon. medical officer; Miss Reid, matron.

Auxilary Home, 59 N. Methven St—Matron, Miss Kerr.

THE FECHNEY INDUSTRIAL SCHOOL.

Certified under Industrial Act 24 & 25 Vict. c. 132.
Instituted 1864.

President—Norman J. Nasmyth, Esq., of Glenfarg.

Vice-President.

A. Ure Wotherspoon, Esq., Lord Provost of the City of Perth.

Trustees ex-officiis.

The Right Hon. the Earl of Mansfield, Convener of the County of Perth; A. U. Wotherspoon, Esq., Lord Provost of the City; Alex. Frazer, Esq., Lord Dean of Guild; John Wilson, Esq., K.C., Sheriff of the County; C. P. Boswell, Esq., Sheriff-Substitute; Rev. Walter E. Lee, M.A., minister of the East Church, Perth.

Ordinary Directors.

Mr. J. Lyall Bowie, solicitor; Mr. John Moncrieff, Summerbank; Mr. Robert Halley, 5 Barossa Place; Mr. William F. M'Cash, Cornhill; Mr. Arch. Murray, Logie House; Mr. Alexander Macduff of Bonhard; Mr. Norman J. Nasmyth of Glenfarg; Mr. John Ritchie, Sheriff Clerk; Col. D. M. Smythe of Methven; Mr. Donald Mackenzie, Bank of Scotland; Mr. Melville Gray, Bowerswell; Mrs John Ritchie, Mrs. W. F. M'Cash; Mr. H. J. Bell, C.E.; Mr. J. Moncrieff Wright of Kinmonth; Mr. James Barlas, High Street.

Condie, Mackenzie, & Co., W.S., 75 George Street, secretaries and treasurers; Dr. Robert Stirling, medical officer; Mr. John H. MacBeth, superintendent; Miss Robertson, matron W. Richardson, teacher; Miss B. Richardson, assistant teacher; Mr. W. Bowman, manual instructor; Mr. C. O'Hare, bandmaster.

SOCIETY FOR THE TREATMENT OF CHRONIC DISEASE AND RELIEF OF INCURABLES IN PERTH AND PERTHSHIRE.

Chairman—Colonel D. M. Smythe of Methven.
Vice-Chairman—
Deputy Vice-Chairman—Robert Stirling, Esq., M.D., Atholl Place, Perth.

Committee of Management.

A. Macduff, Esq., of Bonhard; Sheriff Sym; T. R. Moncrieff, Esq., Springland; The Right Hon. the Earl of Moray; W. F. M'Cash, Esq., Cornhill; Major Mercer, Huntingtower; N. J. Nasmyth of Glenfarg; J. Moncrieff Wright of Kinmonth; Melville Gray, Bowerswell; Brig. Gen. W. K. MacLeod, Greenbank; and David Marshall Esq., Perth.

Lady Visitors.

Mrs. Bannerman; The Countess of Moray, Lady Stewart Richardson, Lady Georgina Home Drummond, Mrs. Annandale, Mrs. Cox, Glendoick; Mrs. Ritchie, Miss Smith, and Miss Stirling.

Robert Stirling, M.D., hon. medical officer; Miss Buchanan, matron; Miss J. J. A. Paul, sister-in-charge (of Sanatorium); J. & J. Miller, W.S., secs. and treas.; S. T. Ellison, clerk and cashier, Hillside Homes.

JAMES MURRAY'S ROYAL ASYLUM.

Incorporated by Royal Charter.

Chairman—The Earl of Mansfield.

EX-OFFICIO DIRECTORS.

His Grace the Duke of Atholl, K.T., Lord Lieutenant of the County; J. Condie Stewart Sandeman, Esq., K.C., Sheriff of the County; C. P. Boswell, Esq., Sheriff-Substitute of the County; A. U. Wotherspoon, Esq., Lord Provost of the City of Perth; Alex. Frazer, Esq., Lord Dean of Guild of said City; David Cunningham, Esq., First Bailie of said City; James M'Cash, Esq., Convener of the Trades of Perth; J. Lyall Bowie, Esq., President of the Society of Solicitors, Perth; Rev. P. R. Landreth, West Parish Church, Perth.

LIFE DIRECTORS.

Alex. Macduff Esq. of Bonhard; The Right Hon. the Earl of Mansfield Norman J. Nasmyth, Esq.. of Glenfarg; Lieut.-Col. J. P. Nisbet Hamilton Grant, D.S.O., Drummonie.

ANNUAL DIRECTORS.

J. Sidney Steel, Esq., of Blackpark, Perth; John Ritchie, Esq., Perth; Sir George Kinloch, of Kinloch, Bart., Meigle; J. Moncrieff Wright, Esq., of Kinmonth, Bridge of Earn; The Very Rev. P. M. Smythe, Braco, Isla Road, Perth, Brig.-Gen. W. K. M'Leod, C.S.I., Greenbank, Perth; Col. J. A. G. R. Drummond Hay of Seggieden, Perth; Walter Mitchell, Esq., Commercial Bank, Perth; The Right Hon. Lord Forteviot; J. G. Farquharson, Esq., National Bank, Perth; Capt. D. A. Taylor of Ballendrick, Bridge of Earn; Major Lewis Gibson, D.S.O., Union Bank, Perth.

COMMITTEE OF MANAGEMENT

Earl of Mansfield; Lord Provost Wotherspoon; Alex. Macduff, Esq.; Norman J. Nasmyth, Esq.; Lieut.-Col. Grant; J. Sidney Steel, Esq.; J. Moncrieff Wright Esq.; The Very Rev. Provost Smythe.

Condie, Mackenzie & Co., W.S., Perth, secretaries and treasurers.
J. & R. Morison & Co., C.A., Perth, auditors.
Walter D. Chambers, M.A., M.D., physician superintendent.
Rev. John W. Henderson, B.D., chaplain.
Miss Rankin, matron. Andrew Emslie, storekeeper.

County Lists.

ABERFELDY.

A Burgh under Police Act, 1891. The Most Honourable The Marquis of Breadalbane, K.G., is Superior, and now grants Feu Charters instead of the old Building Leases of 99 years' duration. The Burgh is situated in the parish of Dull. Population 1592.

Magistrates—Provost, J. D. Haggart; Bailies, C. Munro and J. M'Laren; Clerk to Town Council, A. Clow, Solicitor; Treasurer and Collector, A. Clow.

Resident Justices of the Peace—Marquis of Breadalbane; Alex. Campbell, farmer, Borland; J. Mackay, M.D., Aberfeldy; Provost Haggart, Aberfeldy; J. Scott, Eastertyre, Aberfeldy; Chas. Munro, banker, Aberfeldy; and Peter Anderson, farmer, Duneaves.

Teachers—Aberfeldy Public School, Alex. Grieve, M.A., headmaster; W. G. Folkharde and J. Reid, assistants; Infant School, Miss Chayne, headmistress.

Horticultural Society—Stewart Robertson, Esq. of Edradynate, president; A. A. Macgregor, hon. secretary.

Angling Club—Marquis of Breadalbane, patron; J. Haggart, secretary.

Curling Club (Breadalbane)—Marquis of Breadalbane, patron; C. Munro, preses; A. Clow, solicitor, secretary and treas.

Churches—United Free—Rev. John Macrae, M.A., minister; Congregational—Rev. A. S. Guild; Aberfeldy Parish Church—Rev. C. W. Hutchison, minister; Catholic—Rev. John Coogan, priest (Strathtay).

Aberfeldy Cemetery Co.—P. MacDonald, gardener, gravedigger.

Billposter and Bellman—E. H. Chalmers.

Sheriff Small Debt Court—The small-debt circuit court is held on the last Saturdays of March, July, and November; Charles Munro, sheriff-clerk depute.

Medical Men—John Mackay, M.D., F.R.C.S.E., and Douglas Mackay, M.D.; Dr. P. Campbell. Pharmaceutical chemist—H. B. M'Naughton.

Banks—The Bank of Scotland, John Fergusson, agent. The Union Bank, Charles Munro and W. Munro, joint-agents; Commercial Bank, A. MacDonald.

Registrar of Births, Marriages, and Deaths—D. Thomson merchant.

Inspectors of Poor—Of Dull parish, Jas. MacDonald, Aberfeldy; and of Weem Parish, James Morgan, Aberfeldy.

Posting Establishment—James Menzies, Dunkeld Street.

Carting Contractors—James Menzies; D. M'Lean; and J. Smith & Sons

Registered Plumber—A. & J. Menzies.

Wordie & Co.'s Carrier—Donald M'Laren.

Golf Club—H. M. Wood, secretary.

Aberfeldy Bowling Club—P. M'Kercher, president; Chas. Dawson, secretary.

Gas Company—William Munro, secretary and treasurer.

Post Office and Savings Bank—Miss Pirie, Postmistress.

Stamp Office—   Do.   do.

Excise—R. W. Relleen.

County Constable—Sergeant Gatherum.

Young Women's Christian Association—Mrs. M'Rae, president; Miss J. A Simpson, secretary.

Hotels—Breadalbane Arms—R. MacIntyre; Station Hotel, R. Menzies Palace Hotel, Mrs. Bain; Reid's Crown Temperance.

Home for the Sick—Mrs. Douglas of Killiechassie and John Fergusson, managers.

Railway—To and from Perth four times daily; to Inverness and the north twice daily; stationmaster, John MacGregor.

Carrier—To Fortingall and Glenlyon, D. Fraser.

Markets—October, Thursday before Doune Tryst in November.

Cattle Sales—Thursdays in the Auction Mart. Messrs. M'Donald, Fraser, & Co., Perth, auctioneers.

Football Club—C. L. Stewart, secretary.

Tennis Club—W. Bain, secy. and treasurer.

Mails—Kenmore, Fortingall, and Glenlyon, 8.30 a.m.; England, Edinburgh, Perth, &c., 12.5, 4.30, and 9 p.m. Deliveries—Kenmore, Fortingall, South, generally, 9 a.m.; and 6 p.m.

Breadalbane Highland Gathering—C. J. D. Munro, Union Bank of Scotland, secretary and treasurer.

Falls of Moness (Free to Visitors)—Entrance opposite Breadalbane Arms Hotel.

Public Reading Room, Town Hall Buildings; secretary—Jas. Morgan, Bank of Scotland; treasurer, Robt. Anderson, Bank Street; caretaker, J. M. Allan.

Secretary Local Lodge of Freemasons—John Robertson.

Market Gardeners—P. Macdonald, Kenmore Street, and A. Menzies, Chapel Street.

ABERNETHY

Contains two villages—Abernethy and Aberargie. Population of Parish, 1267. A great resort for summer visitors during July, August, and September. The hills in the vicinity are all open to the public for walking, provided dogs do not accompany to disturb sheep and cattle, and there are some delightful spots for picnics. Glen Abernethy is close to the village, and Glenfarg about a mile and a half to the west. On what is known as the Castle Law, the remains of a Pictish fort has been laid bare. A few of the inhabitants in summer are employed on the fishings on the Tay and Earn. There is good rod fishing in the Farg, which is open. Fruit cultivation is extensively carried on in the district.

Resident Justices of the Peace—W. Peddie, *ex-officio.*

Clergy—Established, Rev. George M'Dougall; United Free, Rev. Arch. H. Taylor.

Teachers—D. S. Mitchell; Miss D. Anderson, infant school.

County Councillors—Archibald Powrie, for Burgh.

Town Council—Wm. Munro, solicitor, town clerk.

Chairman, Parish Council—Major Williamson.

Inspector of Poor and Registrar—D. S. Mitchell

Session-Clerk—David Scott, licensed grocer, Abernethy

Chairman of Heritors' Committee—Major Williamson, Clunie

Heritors' Clerk—Condie, Mackenzie, & Co., Perth

Abernethy Bowling Club—John Morrison, secretary; James Gray, treasurer.

Abernethy Total Abstinence Society — President, Rev. Arch. H. Taylor, M.A.

Provost—Wm. Peddie, postmaster.

Medical Officer of Health—Dr. Stewart, Perth

Linen Works—Messrs Ireland & Wishart, Limited

Sexton—Mitchell Kemp

Underclothing Factory—R. Clow & Co.

Hotel and Hiring—David Brown. Hotel—John Scotland, Ferryfield. Chartered ferry to cross from Strathearn to opposite side of Tay and Earn where the two rivers join

Innkeepers—Mrs James Neville and Eric Gilzean; Baiglie Inn Refreshment Association, Ltd.,

Williamson Hall—James Gray, treas.; John Sandilands, secy.

Fair—Fourth Wednesday of May, day after observed as the "Queen's Birthday" Holiday

Postal Arrangements—Abernethy 2 deliveries and 4 despatches; Aberargie, which is under Abernethy, has 2 deliveries and 2 despatches. Rural Messenger leaving Abernethy, 9 a.m. and 6.30 p.m. Returning from Aberargie, 11.30 a.m. and 7.30 p.m. The Aberargie delivery includes Kilnockie Bank and Crossgates in the first delivery only

Shopkeepers' Half-Holiday—Wednesday.

ALYTH

Erected into a Burgh of Barony by James III. in 1488. Population of town, 1860, and parish, 1077, at last census (1911), total 2937. The chief trade is the manufacture of jute. There is also a woollen manufactory and carding mill doing a large business, with a commodious preserve factory (presently unoccupied).

Resident Justices of the Peace—Sir James H. Ramsay of Bamff, Bart.; John L. Alexander, Geo. Gordon, J. F. Murray, John Yeaman, A. M. Ferguson, D. A. Sandilands, and Provost Inglis, *ex officio.*

Ministers—Rev. J. Meikle, B.D., Established; Rev. James Holburn, South United Free; Rev. John Haggart, North U.F.; Rev. Father Stretch (Blairgowrie), Catholic; Episcopal (vacant).

Loyal Public Library—Open every Monday and Thursday Librarian—Miss Welch.

Banks—Royal Bank of Scotland, John Yeaman, agent; North of Scotland and Town and County Bank, Limited, A. M. Ferguson, agent; Savings Bank, A. M. Ferguson.

Medical Men—Drs. Shaw, M.B., C.M., and Neil MacCallum, M.B., C.M.

Veterinary Surgeons—Murray Lornie, M.R.C.V.S., and A. Thain Kay, M.R.C.V.S.

Heritors' Clerk—James Hill, clerk; C. D. Mitchell, assistant, Registrar—C. D. Mitchell.

School Management Committee—Rev. James Meikle, chairman; D. S. Kidd, clerk.

Public Schools—(St. Andrew Street) D. B. Lawson, M.A., headmaster; John Reid, Jr.; Miss Tod, Miss Sinclair, Miss Blyth, Miss Coldwell, Miss Spark, Miss Green, Miss Geddes, Miss Meldrum; (Gauldswell School), Miss Stirling.

Auctioneers—Scott & Graham, Ltd., Forfar; W. L. Mitchell.

Curling Club—Instituted 1815; admitted into the Royal Caledonian Curling Club, 1848; patron, Earl of Airlie, M.C.; president, W. J. Smith; vice-president, D. B. Lawson; secy., Geo. Patton, Airlie Street; treasurer, D. S. Kidd, solicitor.

Bowling Club—President, Bailie Carruthers; vice-president C. D. Mitchell; secretary, W. M. Stewart; treasurer, L. D. M'Arthur.

Masonic Lodge St. Ninian 732—P. L. Storrier, R.W.M. secretary—C. D. Mitchell

Gas Company—John Yeaman, secretary and treasurer; Arch Coubrough, gas manager.

Hotels—Mrs Eddington, Commercial; Airlie Arms; James M. Wood, Losset; and Wm. Barron, Toutie Street.

Markets—Tuesday preceding 28th May and Tuesday preceding 28th November.

Town Council—W. B. Inglis, provost; Bailies Carruthers and M'Pherson.

Councillors—Inglis, Carruthers, Mitchell, Howe, Newbigging, Buick, Cochrane, and M'Pherson; John Yeaman, clerk and collector; W. Ritchie Smith, Depute; D. S. Kidd, chamberlain; Burgh Prosecutor, D. S. Kidd; Medical Officer of Health, Dr. Sinclair, Forfar; Sanitary Inspector and Burgh Surveyor, John Pennycook.

Solicitors—Messrs. Japp & Yeaman, Market Square (John Yeaman); D. S. Kidd, Airlie St.; A. M. Ferguson, Airlie Street; W. Ritchie Smith, Market Square.

Alyth and Meigle Liberal Association—President, J. F. Murray; secretary, Thomas W. Todd.
Alyth and Meigle Constitutional Association—Hon. President, Sir J. H. Ramsay, Bart., of Bamff; Secretary,
Parish Council—Chairman, J. F. Murray, J.P.; inspector and collector, C. D. Mitchell; medical officers, Drs. Shaw and MacCallum.
County Councillors—Alyth Burgh, A. M. Fergusn. Landward, J. F. Murray; Sir James H. Ramsay. Bart.
Ancient Order of Foresters—Stewart Robertson, secretary.
Golf Club—Secretary, D. Galloway, Jr.; D. A. Sandilands, captain,

ARNGASK

Clergy—Established, Rev. James Campbell, M.A.; United Free Church, Rev. J. W. Jack, M.A., J.P.
School Board—District Representative, Rev. James Campbell, M.A.
Chairman of Parish Council—G. Wilson Murray, Lochelbank; clerk, Mr. Murphy, Milnathort.
Registrar—Peter Anderson, postmasrer.
Headmaster—H. H. Bonar, O.B.E.
Inspector of Poor—Mr. Murphy, Milnathort.
Sanitary Inspector—Robert Barlas, Bridge of Earn.
Heritors' Clerk—H. H. Bonar, O.B.E.
Public Hall Committee—Chairman, Rev. J. W. Jack, M.A. J.P.; Secretary, A. A. Hutton, St. Ronan's.
Golf Club—Captain, Robert Gentle, C.A., Edinburgh; Secy., Rev. J. W. Jack, M.A.
Post Office—Peter Anderson, postmaster. Letters are delivered twice and despatched twice each day.
Hotels—Glenfarg Hotel, Messrs. M'Arthur, Perth; Lomond Hotel (Temperance), Mrs. Charteris.
Bowling Green—Secretary, James Whyte.
Temperance Association—President, Rev. J. W. Jack, M.A.
Curling Club—James White, secretary.
Naval and Military War Pensions' Representatives—Miss Simpson, Blairstruie, and Rev. J. W. Jack, M.A.
Red Cross Secretary—Miss Simpson, Blairstruie.
Nursing Association—President, Mrs. Hunter, Arngask House; Treasurer, Mrs. Mackarsie, Tennessee; Secretary, Mrs. Castler.
Volunteer Finance Committee—Chairman, John Brotherstone; Secretary, Rev. J. W. Jack, M.A.
War Memorial Committee—Chairman, J. Blair Stephenson; Hon. Secretary and Treasurer, Mrs. Vesey.
Women's Rural Institute—President, Mrs. Hunter, Arngask House; Secretary, Miss Deas.
Recreation Club (affiliated to Red Triangle)—President, H. H. Bonar, O.B.E.; Secretary, Thomas Murray, Lochelbank; Treasurer, Miss Jean Taylor.
Sports Committee—President E. Forsyth; Secretary, Arch. Whyte; Treasurer, Robert Hume.
Lightning Committee (under District Committee)—Messrs. Murray, Jas. Deas, and Jas. Whyte

AUCHTERARDER.

Population of Burgh, - 2294.

Distributor of Stamps—Thomas E. Young, W.S.

Writer to the Signet—Thomas E. Young.

Solicitors—James P. Kennaway, P. H. MacFarlane, J. MacFarlane, James M'Beth, and D. R. Riddle.

Notaries Public—Thomas E. Young, P. H. MacFarlane, and James P. Kennaway.

Resident Justices of the Peace—Sir W. S. Haldane of Foswell; R. Y. Hally, Linden Park; Dr. James Macfee, Coloness House; Andrew T. Reid of Auchterarder House; W. M. Jeffray, solicitor; J. P. Kennaway, solicitor; and John S. M'Culloch, watchmaker. J. P. Kennaway, Depute Clerk of the Peace for Central District.

Town Councillors—Edward R. Wright, Provost; James Cairns, senior bailie; P. H. MacFarlane, junior bailie; Alexander Fordyce, John S. Stewart, Alexander D. Robertson; David Abkley, Rev. John Greeson, and Mrs. Gardiner. J. P. Kennaway, town clerk and clerk of court; James M'Beth, treasurer, collector, and burgh prosecutor.

Conveners of Town Council Committees—Of whole Council and Finance, Provost Wright; of Lighting, Cleansing, and Public Health, Councillor Stewart; of Water and Drainage, Bailie Cairns; of Property, Bailie Macfarlane; and of Housing Committee, Councillor Fordyce.

Clergy—Rev. Robert Gardiner, Established; Rev. Norman Mackenzie, M.A., St. Andrew's United Free; Rev. John Lindsay, M.A., West United Free; Rev. John Greeson, St. Kessog's Episcopal; Rev. Joseph Keenan, (Crieff), Catholic Church; clerk of Established Presbytery; Rev. William Hall, Comrie, clerk of United Free Presbytery.

Gas Light Company—Alexander Fordyce, chairman; P. H. MacFarlane, secretary; J. Kirke, manager.

Banks—Bank of Scotland, Gilbert M'Diarmid, agent; Union Bank of Scotland, Thomas E. Young, agent; Savings Bank, J. P. Kennaway, cashier.

Registrar of Births, Marriages, and Deaths—Archibald M'Niven.

Parish Church Session-Clerk—Alexander Drummond.

Medical Men—Jas. Macfee, L.R.C.S.E.; Robt. Sibbald Forrest, M.B., C.M., (Edinburgh); and James Turner Gunn, M.B., F.R.C.S.E.

Medical Officer (Burgh)—Dr. Dobie, Crieff.

Teachers—John Purdie, headmaster; Miss Nisbet, headmistress.

Parish Council—Wm. M'Donald, clerk and inspector; James M'Beth, collector; Dr. Gunn, medical officer.

Curling Club—Captain Hally, president; Wm. Macdonald, secy.; James M'Beth, treasurer.

Auchterarder Recreation Grounds Company, Limited—William Hally, interim secretary and treasurer.

Bowling Club—Wm. Hally, president; Colonel A. T. Reid, John B. Malcolm, and Wm. Robertson, vice-presidents; John Ross, treasurer; James Reid, secretary.

Golf Club—John C. Dougall, captain; John Mallis, hon. secretary and treasurer.

Hotelkeepers—Mrs. Elliot, Star Hotel; Arthur Anderson, Queen's Hotel; Miss Stewart, Crown Hotel; Robert Laurence, Railway Hotel.

Post Office—E. B. Patterson, sub-postmistress—Despatched from Auchterarder Post Office to the South at 7.45 am., North, 4.30 and 7 p.m.; to the North at 1.30, and 7 p.m. Arrivals from the South, 7 a.m., 3.40 p.m.; from the North 7.15 a.m., 3.40 p.m. Deliveries 7.15 a.m., 3.40 p.m. Mail to London, Box closes 4.30 and 7 p.m. Rural postmen despatched to Trinity Gask, Aberuthven and Gask, Tullibardine, Gleneagles, Coul, Kinkell Bridge, Muirton and Duchally, Cloanden, and Millearne, 7.45 a.m. Sabbaths: Despatches to South at 3.15 p.m.; to the North 7.20 a.m., and 2.30 p.m. No delivery on Sabbaths, but letters may be got at Post Office between the hours of 9 and 10 a.m. Parcel Post despatches 6 a.m., 1.30 and 5.30 p.m. Deliveries 7.15 a.m., and 3.40 p.m.

Telephone Exchange, 7 a.m. to 8.30 p.m.; Public Call Office, 8 a.m. to 7 p.m.; Sundays, 9 to 10 a.m.

Weekly Market—Saturday at 6 p.m.

Auchterarder Institute, open 8 a.m. to 10 p.m.—Chairman of committee, David Arkley; secretary, G L. Maltman; treasurer, Thos. E. Young; manager, John Dewar; Reading Room (free) open all day; Library (free) open on Tuesday, Thursday, and Saturday from 7 to 9 p.m., and on Wednesday and Saturday from 3 to 5 p.m.

Upper Strathearn Combination Poorhouse—Chairman, Provost M'Ainsh, Doune; governor, J. R. Tennent; medical officer, Dr. Forrest; chaplain, Rev. Robert Gardiner, B.D., Auchterarder; Thomas E. Young, secretary and treasurer.

Heritors' Clerk—John Macfarlane.

D. Coy. 6th Battalion The Black Watch (R.H.)

Cricket Club—John Dougall, captain; William Macdonald, secretary; James Duff, treasurer.

Stock Sales—Every alternate Saturday as advertised—Hay & Co., Limited, Perth, salesmen.

Veterinary Surgeon—William Donaldson, M.R.C.V.S.

St. John's Lodge of Freemasons (No. 46)—Right Worshipful Master, Angus Macpherson; John Macfarlane, secretary; A. D. Garrie, treasurer.

Gleneagles Royal Arch Chapter (No. 475)—Z., Wm. Combe; E, D. A. Ramsay; Treas., T. E. Young. Meetings 2nd Tuesday of the month.

County Police—Alexander Malcolm, sergeant.

Ancient Order of Foresters—Chief ranger, James Dunn; surgeon to the Court,, R. S. Forrest, M.B., C.M. (Edin.); secretary, Edward R. Wright; treasurer, James Callum.

Independent Order of Rechabites—" Crook o' Moss " Tent, R. Tran, chief ruler; D. C. Dewar, secretary; W. Tran, treasurer; Dr. Forrest, surgeon.

Independent Order of Good Templars—" Excelsior " Lodge.

Horticultural Society—T. E. Young, President; Thos. M'Arly, Vice-President; Thomas L. Anderson, Vice-President; D. Rodger, Secretary; and James Duff, Treasurer.

Unionist Association—Græme A. L. Whitelaw, President; Colonel A. T. Reid, Vice-President; P. H. MacFarlane, Secretary and Treasurer.

Literary Society—Miss Haldane, Hon. President; Rev. John Greeson, President; S. Young, Secretary; and Miss Knight, Treasurer.

Dramatic Society—Andrew Martin, President; W. R. Cairns, Secretary; and Charles M'Intyre, Treasurer.

Town Band—Auchterarder Town Council.

Bible Society—Rev. John Greeson, President; Thomas E. Young, Secretary; and Gilbert M'Diarmid, Treasurer.

Scotch Girls' Friendly Society—Mrs. Haldane, President; Mrs. Young and Miss Henderson, Joint-Secretaries.

Highland Gathering—James Dow, Jr., Secretary.

County Councillor—J. P. Kennaway, Solicitor.

Station Agent—Thomas M. Roy.

Sanitary Inspector—Thomas Thomson.

Burgh Inspector and Burgh Surveyor—Thomas Thomson.

Billposter—D. M'Nab.

BIRNAM.

Resident Justices of the Peace—W. Steuart Fothringham of Murthly; James Paton. Obney; James Scott, Birnam.

Ministers—Rev. Charles M. Robertson, M.A., Established; Rev. William Gwyther, St. Mary's Episcopal; Rev. J. M'Ainsh, Strathbraan, United Free; Rev. John Coogan (Strathtay), Catholic.

Medical Practitioners—Dr. J. A. Mathers and Dr. Taylor.

Public School—Chas. A. Lunan, M.A., headmaster; Miss Ramsay, Miss Finlayson and Miss Hamilton, assistants.

School Management Committee—Duchess of Atholl, Mrs. Dow, Mrs. Millar, Rev. J. M'Ainsh (chairman), Rev. C. M. Robertson, Rev. J. Hamilton, Rev. K. O. M'Leod, Mr. A. Campbell, Mr. H. Crombie, Arthur Harris, clerk and treasurer.

Parish Council—W. A. Rae, chairman; Messrs. Robertson, Murthly; Anderson, Ballinloan; Wm. Anderson, Birnam; Keir, Ladywell; Fraser, Birnam; Rev. John M'Ainsh, Strathbraan; Rev. C. M. Robertson, Little Dunkeld Manse; Joseph Sim, Birnam.

Birnam Highland Games held annually—Colonel Steuart Fothringham of Murthly, Patron; Arthur Harrison, vice-president; James M'Intosh, secretary; Alex. Campbell, treasurer.

Rohallion and Birnam Curling Club—Colonel Steuart Fothringham of Murthly, patron; Mrs. W. S. Fothringham, patroness; D. Fraser, president; Arthur Harris, treasurer and secretary; J. M'Leish and A. F. Mackenzie, representative members.

County Councillor—Colonel Steuart Fothringham of Murthly

Railway (Highland)—A Fraser, station-master.

Post, Telegraph, and Savings Bank Office—Charles John Low.

Letter Carriers—Charles Morgan and J. Stewart.

Inspector of Poor and Collector—Arthur Harris.

Registrar—C. J. Low.

Gas Work—W. F. Doble, chairman; John Purdie and David Keir, directors; A. Campbell, secretary and treasurer; John M'Donald, manager.

County Police—Alex. Balfour.

Birnam Institute—Rev. Wm. Gyther, president; John Jackson, secy. and treasurer; committee, C. A. Lunan, John Stewart, D. Fraser, Rev. C. M. Robertson, Joseph Sim; A. M'Rae, attendant.

Birnam, Dunkeld, and District Nursing Association—President, Duchess of Atholl; Convener, Mrs. Steuart Fotheringham; secretary and treasurer, Mrs. Arthur Harris, Little Dunkeld; Nurses Campbell and Martin.

Birnam and Dunkeld Recreation Ground—Colonel Steuart Fothringham, patron; Rev. T. R. Rutherford, president; R. M'Gillewie, secretary; Dr. Taylor, treasurer.

Dunkeld and Birnam Whist Club—A. F. Mackenzie, president; A. Buchanan, secretary and treasurer

Hotels—Birnam Hotel, Roderick Gillies.

Birnam Unionist Association—Colonel Steuart Fothringham, president; A. Campbell, Beechwood, Birnam, secretary and treasurer.

Birnam and Dunkeld Red Cross Society, Women's Detachment—Miss Bulloch, Commandant; Men's Detachment Col. M'Donald, Commandant.

Birnam and Dunkeld Bowling Club—Colonel Steuart Fothringham of Murthly, patron; J. Crombie, president; T. Buchanan, secretary and treasurer.

BLACKFORD.

Resident Justices of the Peace—J. R. Sharp, Viewfield, and Jas. M. Taylor, boot manufacturer.

Ministers—Parish Church, seated for 632. Peter Milne, B.D. United Free, seated for 500. D. S. M'Lachlan, M.A.

Session-Clerk—George Eadie. Postmistress—Miss C. A. Fraser.

Surgeon—   Registrar—D. Richards, M.A.

Sanitary Inspector—John Wilson

Station-agent—John MacKenzie.

Bank of Scotland Branch—D. S. Stewart, agent

Inspector of Poor and Collector—D. Richards, M.A.

Innkeepers—Alex. Collie, Joseph MacKay.

Moray Arms Hotel—Robert Still; Blackford Hotel—John Barclay.

Gas Light Company—R. M'Intosh, manager

Curling Club—Captain Drummond Moray of Abercairny, patron; president, D. Y. Stewart; secretary and treasurer, A. J. Connal.

Clerk to the Heritors—Wm. Macfarlane

Population of the Parish, 1374; village, 565

Angling Club—   , president; D. Hutcheson, secretary; and J. Connal, treasurer

Bowling Club—James M. Taylor, president; Geo. Ferguson, vice-president.

Schools—Blackford Public, D. Richards, M.A.; Gleneagles, Mrs. Stalker; Tullibardine, Robert Guthrie

Forester's Court—George Eadie, secretary

Moray Institute—D. S. Stewart, int. secretary and treasurer.

Golf Club—James Arnott, secretary

Public Library—John Galloway, librarian.

Parish Council—Capt. W. H. Drummond Moray, chairman; John Stewart, vice-chairman

BLAIR-ATHOLL

Resident Justices of the Peace—The Duke of Atholl, C.B., D.S.O., M.V.O.; Her Grace the Duchess of Atholl, LL.D.; Robert Inglis, Esq., Old Blair.

Clergy—Established, Rev. Donald Lamont, M.A.; U.F., Rev. A. A. Strathearn, M.A.; Episcopal, Rev. D. M'Naught, Pitlochry. Rev. D. Sinclair, Struan.

Heritors' Clerk—A. Kellock

School Board—Chairman, Rev. D. Lamont; clerk, George Forrest, Tullibardine Institute.

Public School—Headmaster—A. Kellock, F.E.I.S.; mistress, Miss Isa E. Allan; assistants, Miss Mary Rousay.

Session-Clerk and Registrar—A. Kellock

Banks—Union Bank, John R. M'Kenzie, agent

Inspector of Poor—Mr. George Forrest.

Veter. Surgeons—John Panton, M.R.C.V.S. Alex. Panton, V.S.

Red Cross, V.A.D.—Secretary, Mr. A. M'Gregor.

United Guild Party—President, Her Grace the Duchess of Atholl; sec., Miss Robertson, "Invergarry."

Post Office—Angus M'Gregor, postmaster. *Despatches* for S.
and E., 6.20 a.m., 12.20 p.m., 5.50 p.m.; N., 8 a.m.
Delivery, 8.55 a.m.
Hotels — Atholl Arms, D. D. Macdonald. Bridge of Tilt,
George J. Christie
Library—A. Kellock, librarian.
Tullibardine Institute—Secretary, Mr. George Forrest
Parish Council—Chairman, Robert Inglis, Esq., Old Blair,
Medical Officer—Dr. Anderson, Pitlochry
Scottish Horse Hall—Cpl. R. Irvine.
Atholl Band of Hope—Superintendent, R. G. Ross.
Rural Workers' Friendly Society—Chairman, Mr. G. Forrest;
secretary, R. G. Ross.
Rifle Club—Mr. W. W. Livingstone, secretary
Temperance Society—President, Rev. D. Lamont, M.A.; secy.,
Rev. A. A. Strathearn, M.A.

BLAIRGOWRIE

Town Council—Thos. N. Tasker, provost ; Thos. K. Dewar
and Thos. M'Kenzie, bailies ; Walter Davidson, A. Ander-
son, S. A. Lamb, P. S. Robertson, A. Spalding, James B
M'Gibbon, Robert Gunn, Frank Turnbull, and Alexander
Fyffe, councillors ; Wm. Keay, town clerk.
The Blairgowrie, Rattray, and District Water Board—By the
Town Council—Provost Tasker, Bailie Dewar, Bailie
M'Kenzie, and Councillors P. S. Robertson, A. Spalding,
and F. Turnbull. By the Town Council of Rattray—
Provost Wm. Scott, Bailie Thomson, and Bailie Proctor.
By the District Committee—Mr. Wm. Falconer, Mr. Robert
Clark, and Mr. James Ritchie.
Burgh Surveyor and Sanitary Inspector—Mr. W. D. M. Falconer
Inspector of Police—   Mitchell,
Clerk to Local Authority and Police Clerk—William Keay.
Police Court—criminal offences—every lawful day at 9.30 a.m.
—J B. Begg, fiscal.
Sheriff Court—The small-debt court held quarterly for cases
under £20, on the second Saturday of January, and first
Saturday of April, July, and October—J. B. Miller, depute-
clerk
Inland Revenue Officer—Donald M'Donald
Resident Justices of the Peace—A. W. Bennett, Alex. Reid, P. S.
Robertson, J. B. Miller, J. M. Hodge, R. R. Black ; Chas.
Boyd, Solicitor, Coupar-Angus, depute-clerk.
Solicitors—R. Robertson Black, J. B. Miller, J. B. Gerrard,
J. P. Noble, J. W. Young, J. M. Hodge, John Stewart, Wm.
Keay, J. B. Begg.
Notaries Public—J. B. Miller, R. Robertson Black, Wm. Keay,
and J. P. Noble.
Auctioneer—Robert Reid
Inspector of Poor and Registrar—Jas. S. Brown
Collector of Poor Rates—Jas. S. Brown

D.

Collector of Police Rates—William Keay

Stamp Distributor—J. B. Miller, solicitor

Medical Men—Thomas A. F. Hood and Peter Shaw

Veterinary Surgeons—W. Nairn

Bankers—A. Gemmell, Commercial Bank; A. W. Henderson, bank of Scotland; W. H. Cromarty, Union Bank of Scotland; David Mitchell and Fred. Will, Royal Bank of Scotland; W. Craigie, Savings Bank; I. Watt, North of Scotland and Town and County Bank

Gas Light Company—Committee of Management—John Smith, chairman; D. Adamson, Wm. Collie, Wm. Melville, A. C. Milne, Andrew Spalding, Wm. Stewart. Clerk and Treas. —John Stewart, Rattray.

Ardblair Curling Club—J. P. Noble, secretary; Geo. Wyllie treasurer; Adam Hill, president

Curling Club—Dr. P. W. Shaw, president; D. W. Scott, vice-president; W. T. Robertson, secretary; P. J. Robertson, treasurer.. Repres. members, T. N. Tasker and R. Gunn

Bowling Club—Mr. James Fleming, president; Mr. Alex. Stiven, vice-president; Mr. T. K. Dewar, secretary; Mr. P. K. M'Intosh, treasurer

Hotels—Royal, Alf Fairs; Queen's, Robert Gunn; Station, D. Ogilvie; Temperance, G. Sharpe; Victoria, E. Mackintosh; Railway, J. Kolher

Live Stock Sales held every alternate Tuesday

Fairs and Markets—Macdonald, Fraser, & Co. hold a regular fat stock sale every second Tuesday; spring and autumn sales of store cattle (generally on a Thursday, Feeing markets are fixed and advertised by Town Council. Fair o' Blair, first Tuesday after fourth Monday in July

Session-Clerks—Parish of Blairgowrie, J. W. Young; St. Mary's, Blairgowrie, John Templeton.

CALLANDER.

A Burgh under Police Act, 1862.--Population in 1911, 1504.

Resident Justices of the Peace—Thomas Macdonald, Ach-na-Coile, Callander; Alexander Scott, Kintillo House; Donald M'Laren, Chairman of Parish Council; John Stewart, solicitor, Dunblane, depute clerk of the peace.

Parish Council—Donald M'Laren, chairman; James Macdonald, clerk

Postmaster—Donald Mackenzie.

Stamp Office—Post Office.

Banks—Bank of Scotland, R. S. Potts, agent; Wm. Bennett teller. Commercial Bank, M'Michael and Buchanan, agents; Jas. Pritchard, accountant; Savings Bank, Donald M'Laren, cashier

Medical Men—Wm. Harvey M.B., C.M.; Alfred J. Beattie, M.B., C.M.

Hotelkeepers—Dreadnought Hotel, Dreadnought Hotel Coy., Ltd.; Ancaster Arms, James Mitchell; Crown Hotel, Arch. Menzies; Caledonian (Temperance), W. Mackay; other Temperance Hotels, Misses Duncan, Mrs. Stewart, Mr. Deans, Mrs. Simpson; Callander Hydropathic, Colonel Scott, Proprietor; Mr. and Mrs. Rathie, managers·

Clergymen—Rev. T. Burnett Peter. B.D., Parish; Rev. R. E. M'Intyre, U.F.; Rev. H. L. Skinner, Episcopal.

Solicitors—M'Michael & Buchanan, Donald M'Laren.

Notaries Public—Peter Buchanan and Donald M'Laren.

Registrar—James M'Donald, inspector of poor.

Session Clerk—Donald M'Laren, solicitor.

Gas Company—J. M'Michael, secy. and treas.; J. Bell, manager

Town Council—M. V. Dow, provost; Richard Williamson, bailie; A. D. Cumming, bailie.

Town Clerk—Peter Buchanan.

Burgh Chamberlain—Donald M'Laren, solicitor.
Burgh Fiscal—John Mill,

Inspector of Poor—James Macdonald.

Burgh Manager—Wm. Nicol.

Public Hall—Peter Buchanan, secretary.

School Management Committee—Thos. Macdonald, J.P., chairman; Donald M'Laren, clerk.

M'Laren High School—James Leckie, M.A., rector; Thomas Macdonald, chairman of managers; D. M'Laren, clerk.

M'Laren Educational Trust—D. M'Laren of Bracklinn, chairman of Governors; Donald M'Laren, clerk, treasurer, and factor.

Public School—A. D. Cumming, F.S.A., headmaster.

Callander Curling Club — Archibald Menzies, president; Duncan Stewart, , secretary and treasurer.

Callander Junior Curling Club—D. M'Laren of Bracklinn, president; Peter Buchanan, seretary.

Callander Golf Club—Wm. M Ewen, captain; John Mill, secy.

Ladies' Golf Club—Miss C. MacEwan, secretary.

Callander Bowling Club—P. M. Macintyre, president; A. Menzies, vice-president; A. D. Cumming, secy.; A. Menzies, treas.

Masonic—Lodge Ben Ledi (No. 614), G. Dyet, R.W.M.; John Glen, treasurer.

Heritors' Clerk—Peter Buchanan.

Boys' Brigade—Archibald Kay, R.S.W., captain; D. M'Niven, lieutenant.

Callander Abstainers' Union—J. Macdonald, treasurer.

Callander Amenity Committee — Provost Dow, chairman; John M'Michael, secretary; P. M. Macintyre, treasurer.

Primrose League—J. E. Crabbie, advocate, ruling councillor; Miss Annie C. Grieve, secretary.

Callander Nursing Society—Thomas Macdonald, president; Donald M'Laren, secretary and treasurer.

Callander Institute—Viscount Esher, president; P. M. Macintyre, vice-president; James Macdonald, secretary.

Red Triangle Club—A. D. Cumming, chairman; T. H. Kennedy, secretary.

Bible Society—Thomas Macdonald, president; Rev. William Wilson, Rev. R. E. M'Intyre, and Rev. T. B. Peter, vice-presidents; Donald M'Laren, secretary and treasurer.

Young Men's Christian Association—A. D. Cumming, F.S.A., chairman; Jas. Macdonald, treasurer.

Scottish Girls' Friendly Society (Callander Branch)—Miss Jessie Grieve, hon. secretary.

Sanitary Inspector—W. N. Nicol.

Callander and District Unionist Association—D. M'Laren of Bracklinn, president; Donald M'Laren, secretary and treasurer.

Callander and District Liberal Association—John Barlow, M.D., F.R.C S., president.

Callander Angling Club—John Roberts, Rock Villa, president; Wm. Imrie, secretary.

Callander Cycle Club—Peter Clark, secretary.

Callander Tennis Club—J. M'Michael, secretary.

Callander Badminton Club—Mrs. Roberts, Rock Villa, Captain.

COMRIE.

Clergy—Rev. A. B. Wann, D.D., Established; Rev. Arthur Crawford Watt, M.A., West U.F.; Rev. Wm. Hall, East U.F.; Rev. Mr. Brown, Episcopal Church.

Teachers—James Goldie, public; Miss Elder, St. Fillans; Miss Ritchie, Glenlednock; Miss Luke, Glenartney.

School Management Committee—P. M'Intyre, Esq., Tighnablair, chairman; John P. Mitchell, clerk.

Medical—C. D. Temple, M.B., C.M.

Banks—Commercial Bank, J. A. Masson.

Inspector for the Poor—J. P. Mitchell, solicitor.

Clerk to Heritors—J. P. Mitchell, solicitor.

Clerk to Kirk-Session—David Richard.

Postmistress—Miss Miller.

Registrar—J. P. Mitchell, solicitor.

Lawers and Comrie Curling Clubs—Rev. C. D. R. Williamson, preses; David Richard, treasurer and secretary.

Monzievaird and Strowan—C. H. Graham Stirling of Strowan, president; J. G. Moncur, secretary.

Masonic Lodge (St. Kessac's)—T. Miller, R.W.M.; P. Macpherson, secretary.

County Police—A. M'Naughton, Comrie.

Sanitary Inspector—John K. Robertson.

Innkeepers—Royal Hotel, Miss Brown; Ancaster Hotel, D. Millar; Temperance Hotel, Miss Stirling; Commercial Temperance, Mrs. M'Nicoll, Drummond Arms. St. Fillans. Mr. R. A. Campbell.

Insurance Agents—Sun Fire Office, R. C. Risk; Edinburgh Life Assurance Co. and Alliance Assurance Companies, J. H. Masson, banker; General Accident, N.B. and Mercantile, Royal Life Association, John P. Mitchell.

Dundas Public Library—Mrs. M'Lagan, House of Ross, president; James Goldie, secretary.

Comrie Reading-Room—J. P. Mitchell, chairman;

Comrie War Memorial Institute—Chairman, secretary,

Horticultural and Industrial Association—J. Gilbert, secretary; P. Macpherson, treasurer.

Primrose League—J. Stobie, secretary; Hon. Mrs. Williamson, Lawers, ruling councillor.

Pigeon and Poultry Association—D. Millar, secretary.

Scotch Girls' Friendly Society—Miss Morison, Milton, Comrie, secy

Parish Council—Major C. H. G. Stirling of Strowan, chairman; members—J. Williamson, John Carmichael, Peter Macpherson, H. M'Kinstry, J. Strachan, D. M'Intyre, D. Kay.

County Council—J. P. Mitchell, Esq., representative.

Good Templar Lodge—"Royal Oak,"

Golf Club—T. Miller, treasurer; J. Goldie, secretary.

Comrie Liberal Unionist Association—Sir G. W. M. Dundas, president; D. R. W. Kemp, secretary.

Liberal Association—John Robertson, secretary.

Posting Masters—Duncan Comrie, P. M'Dougall, R. A. Campbell, St. Fillans. Motors: R. A. Campbell, St Fillans; G. M'Nab, Comrie; Wm. J. M'Rostie.

Comrie Public Hall—Parish Council.

Comrie Band of Hope and Bible Class Temperance Society—Miss G. Boyd, secretary.

Comrie Orchestral Society—T. Miller, secretary.

COUPAR-ANGUS

Coupar-Angus Linen Works—Durie & Miller.

Strathmore Linen Works—The Strathmore Linen Co., Limited.

Strathmore Printing Works—W. Culross & Son.

Strathmore Tannery—George Honeyman & Son.

Turning Works—Balgersho Engineering Works, D. Murray; and J. Lindsay, Queen Street.

Coupar-Angus Preserve Works—John Fleming & Sons.

Postmistress—Miss Easton.

Stamp Office, National Bank Buildings—C. Boyd, sub-distributor

Banks—Union Bank, James Bell, agent; National Bank, C. Boyd; Bank of Scotland, W. Irvine, agent; Savings Bank—David Culross, agent.

Public School—G. W. F. Strain, headmaster.

Ministers—Rev. Charles Stewart, M.A., B.D., Established; Rev. T. Goldie, M.A., South United Free; Rev. John Walker, North United Free; Congregational Union (vacant); Rev. Seton Deuchar, Episcopal.

Y.W.C.A.—President, Miss Walker; Miss Irvine, treasurer.

Medical—Jas. Muckart; H. A. C. Davidson, L.R.C.P.S.. Ed.
Solicitors and Notaries Public—C. Boyd, R. Watson, and J.
    Adam.
Registrar of Births, Marriages, and Deaths—R. K. Macintyre.
Police Constables—John Reid and Robert Wallace.
Poor Rates—R. K. Macintyre, inspector and collector.
Innkeepers—Royal Hotel, W. R. Robertson; Railway Hotel,
    T. Craig; Strathmore Hotel, W. Aitken; Victoria Inn,
    Hugh Mackay; Atholl Arms, Mrs M'Farlane.
Police Magistrates—Thomas Stuart, provost; James Bruce and
    Henry Cobb, bailies.
Town Councillors—Wm. Dunbar, D. Murray, L. Anderson,
    W. Anderson, and J. Lindsay.
Parish Council—R. K. Macintyre, inspector, &c.
Gas Company—R. Watson, clerk and treasurer; J. Brodie,
    manager.
Town Clerk—Robert Watson.
    R. Reid, Burgh Surveyor.   F. Galloway, Water Inspector.
Collector and Treasurer—R. K. Macintyre
Halls—Victoria—Wm. Macintosh, hall-keeper.   Royal—W. R.
    Robertson, proprietor.
Veterinary Surgeon—Mr. William Clark, F.R.C.V.S.
Procurator-Fiscal—C. Boyd.   J.P. Clerk-Depute—C. Boyd.
Heritors' Clerk—C. Boyd.
Railway Agents—Caledonian Railway, James Williamson.
Road Surveyor for Eastern District of Perthshire—George
    Wyllie, Duan Villa, Blairgowrie.
Markets—Weekly grain market, Thursday.
Curling Club—William Whitson of Isla Park, president;
    R. Anderson and L. B. Mills, joint sec. and treas
Bowling Club—R. K. Macintyre, president; R. K. Macintyre,
    secretary and treasurer.
Horticultural Society—J. Simpson, secretary; J. Johnstone,
    assistant secretary and treasurer.
Masonic—Lodge St. John's, No. 105—F. Bradley, jr., R.W.M.;
    R. K. Macintyre, Bellevue, secretary; Rev. J. Walker, treas.
Ancient Order of Foresters—D. Smith, chief ranger; G. Bur-
    nett, secretary; L. Macfarlane, treasurer.
Reporters—A. S. Erskine, *Dundee Advertiser*, etc.; *Dundee
    Courier* and *Evening Telegraph, etc.*
Comrades of the Great War—J. Lundie, chairman; T. Coegan,
    secretary; T. Brown, treasurer.

CRIEFF.

Resident Justices of the Peace—Earl of Ancaster, Sir Patrick
    Keith Murray, Bart., of Ochtertyre; Captain William A. S.
    H. Drummond Moray of Abercairny; R. T. N. Speir of
    Culdees, Muthill; Capt. Julian Colquhoun of Clathick;

A. G. Maxtone Graham of Cultoquhey; C. H. Graham Stirling of Strowan; R. M'Naughtan of Cowden; A. O. Newbigging of Dalchonzie, D. Keith Murray, W. H. Mungall, S. Drysdale, Henry Campbell, Archibald Adie, John M'Nee, W. E. Frost, Alex. Kerr, Arch. Millar, D. Hardie, Rev. H. H. Murray, James M'Ara, M. H. P. Watt, J. P. Kennaway, solicitor, Auchterarder, depute-clerk.

Police Commissioners—Walter Heggie Mungall, provost; Jas. Tainsh, senior bailie; Peter M'Owan, junior bailie; John Scrimgeour, James Reid, Malcolm Finlayson, Wm. Watts, F. N. Hunt, Wm. Brown, D. F. Ferguon, commissioners; C. E. Colville, clerk; C. D. M. Ross, fiscal; William Pickard, collector;   burgh surveyor; Police Court every lawful day.

School Management Committee—Members—J. M. Taylor, S Graham Mickel, Rev. H. H. Murray, Mrs. M'Lagan, J. H. Brown, John Gow, Rev. Joseph Keenan, Rev. Canon Meredith, F. N. Hunt, George T. Ewing, James Lennox, Malcolm Finlayson, clerk.

Schools—Commissioner Street, J. H. Brown, headmaster; Miss Clark, industrial department; Taylor's Institution, W. Reid, headmaster; Monzie and Innerpeffray.

Parish Council—Chairman, John Dinwoodie; inspector and registrar, P. G. M'Ara.

Heritors of Crieff—Clerk, James MacRosty.

Central District Committee of County Council—Chairman, The Right Hon. The Earl of Mansfield, Scone Palace; clerk and collector Malcolm Finlayson; surveyor, Alex. Roberton.

Clergymen—Andrew Campbell, M.A., St. Michaels; Rev. A. Heggie, West Church; A. Henderson, D.D., Rev. Hunter Smith, M.A., Rev. James Ferguson, B.D., U.F.; M'Cubbin, Congregational; Wm. R. Simpson, Baptist; W. M. Meredith, Episcopalian; Father Joseph Keenan, Roman Catholic.

Medical—Jas. Gairdner, Coldwells; M. Burnet, Beech Knowes; A. Stuart, Ivy Lodge; W. Haig, Galvelmore; D. R. Dobie, James Square.

Solicitors—Malcolm Finlayson, C. E.Colville, S. Drysdale, T. M'Duff, C. D. M. Ross, S. G. Mickel, James MacRosty, and James Reid.

Notaries Public—Malcolm Finlayson, S. Drysdale, and James MacRosty.

Sheriff Small-Debt Court—Held first Saturday of March, June, September and December—Malcolm Finlayson, depute-clerk.

Bank Agents—Bank of Scotland, R. Allan; British Linen, J. Robertson; Commercial, T. B. M'Naughton; Union, J. Dinwoodie; Clydesdale, C. R.Fleming; North of Scotland, M. H. P. Watt; Savings, J. Dinwoodie.

Morrison's Academy—Governors, Professor Paterson, Rev. Dr. Henderson, S. Drysdale, Rev. H. H. Murray, G. T. Ewing, Rev. A. Campbell, Provost Mungall, J. P. Kennaway and

Miss Haldane of Clioan; local clerk, M. Finlayson, solicitor.
Boys' School, Alexander Wright, rector. Girls' School—
Miss Mason, lady superintendent.

Taylor's Trust Free Library—Governors—S. G. Mickel, J.
Tainsh, M. Finlayson, J. MacRosty, clerk.

Private School—Dalvreck, W. E. Frost, headmaster.

Teachers of Music—M. Dobinson, Victoria Terrace; Harris,
Ellangowan; Turner, Burrell Street; and Mrs. Yew-
dall, Burrell Street.

Hotelkeepers—Drummond Arms, Bruce Kelly; Commercial,
Mrs. Doyle; Crown, R. Thomas; Station, S. G. M'Donald;
Star, C. M'Donald; Pretoria, Melrose.

Temperance Hotels—H. T. Brett, James Square; Duncan,
James Square.

Veterinary Surgeons—Watt and Beattie.

Excise Officer—James Chalmers.

Gas Company—Dr. Meikle, chairman; William Pickard, treasurer and secretary; J. Napier, manager.

Postmaster—J. M'Kenzie.

Auctioneer—M. D. Stewart.

Newspaper—*Strathearn Herald*-(Saturday morning).

Strathearn Hydropathic Establishment Co. (Ltd.)—Dr. Gordon
Meikle, manager and resident physician.

6th Bat. (Black Watch)—James Reid, captain; Rev. Hunter
Smith, chaplain; Dr. Haig, surgeon.

Masonic Society—Lodge St. Michael's, No. 38—A. Watt Allison,
R.W.M.; T. M'Duff, secretary.

Strathearn Agricultural Society—M. Finlayson, secy. and treas.

Upper Strathearn Curling Province—Malcolm Finlayson, secy.

Crieff Curling Club—James Reid, secretary and treasurer.

Ochtertyre Curling Club—M. H. P. Watt, secy. and treas.

Bowling Club, Ltd.—M. H. P. Watt, treas.;   secy.

Golf Club—Dr. Burnet, captain; T. Paterson, secy.

Foresters' Society—William Pickard, secretary.

Crieff Nursing Assn.—Misses Hope, secs.; H. Campbell, treas.

Cemetery Trust—J. MacRosty, clerk.

DOUNE.

Resident Justices of the Peace—General John H. Campbel
of Inverardoch; Provost M'Anish, and John Main

Postmistress—Margaret Dewar. Stamps at Post Office

Registrar and Session-clerk—William Gray

Heritors' Clerk and Writer—James A. M'Lean, clerk to Commission

Inspector of Poor, Collector of Rates—W. Gray

Public Teachers—Doune—P. C. Merrie, headmaster, and Miss
Sinclair; Deanston—K. S. Murray, headmaster, and Miss
Ramsay,

Veterinary Surgeon—Duncan M'Farlane

Banker—W. D. Thomson, agent for the Union Bank of Scotland, Limited

Savings Bank—At Post Office

Freemasons' Lodge (instituted 1789)—Rev. John Chalmers Peat, B.D., R.W.M.; P. Cuthbert, secretary

Curling Club—The Earl of Moray, president; Gen. Campbell, vice-president; W. M'Anish, secretary and treasurer; representative members, James Buchanan and J. Scrimgeour

Moray Institute—James M'Anish, president; Fred Mungall, treasurer; Ian Campbell, secy. Annual subscription, 5s.

Kilmadock and Kincardine Horticultural Association (instituted 1837)—Earl of Moray, hon. president; W. M'Carrell, convener; secretary and treasurer.

Public Vaccinator—John Reid, medical officer.

Bowling Club—W. M'Anish, president; R. Ferguson, secretary; Wm. A. M'Farlane, treasurer.

School Board—J. M'Anish, chairman; J. A. M'Lean, clerk

Police Constables—Wm. Gordon, R. M'Kenzie.

Doune Agricultural Association—President, Earl of Moray; convener, John Scrimgeour; secretary, William Gray.

Chief Magistrate—James M'Ainsh.

Doune Castle—Custodian, Mr. M'Cutchin.

Doune Golf Club—Earl of Moray, patron; General Campbell, president; Rev. J. C. Peat, captain; P. C. Merrie, secretary; W. M. Gray, treasurer.

DUNBLANE.

Resident Justices of the Peace—Brig.-Gen. Stirling of Keir; J. G. Stewart, Aultwharrie; James Rodger, Keir Mains; A. H. Anderson, The Firs; A. W. Hay Drummond, of Cromlix; Major Murray Stewart, Kinachoile; Charles Chick, Union Bank.

Depute Clerk of the Peace—John Stewart, Solicitor.

Western District Committee of County Council—Chairman, Brig.-Gen. Stirling of Keir; clerk, treasurer, and collector, John Stewart, solicitor; road surveyor, W. L. Gibson, C.E.

Postmaster—Peter Campbell; R. Campbell, Sub-Postmaster Ramoyle. Post Office Savings Bank

County Savings Bank—John Stewart, solicitor, agent.

Banks—Jas. Barty, agent for the Bank of Scotland.
Charles Chick, agent for Union Bank of Scotland, Ltd.

Income-Tax—James Barty, clerk to the commissioners.

Curling Club—John A. Stirling, Esq. of Kippendavie, patron; D. C. Blair, president; James Guthrie, W. P. Tod, W. L. Gibson, Robt. Thomas, and A. H. Anderson, vice-presidents; J. C. Waddell, secretary and treasurer.

Thistle Curling Club—A. W. H. Hay Drummond of Cromlix, patron; R. M'Gregor, pres.; J. Cramb, sec. and treas.

Dunblane Building Co., Limited.—J. A. M'Lean. solicitor, sec. and treas.

Dunblane Co-operative Society, Ltd.—Manager, T. B. Barrie.

Medical—James F. Lindsay, M.B., C.M.; A. C. Buist, M.B.
C.M.; T. Dewar, M.D.

Ministers—Established, The Rev. J. Hutchison Cockburn,
B.D.; Rev. Ed. M. F. M'Hugh, Episcopal; Rev. D. R.
Alexander, B.D., Leighton U.F.C.; Rev. Hugh Stevenson,
M.A., East U.F.C.; and Rev. Canon Dowling (Doune).
Roman Catholic Church.

Queen Victoria Memorial School—Colonel Mitford, commandant; Captain Mackie, Adjutant.

Sheriff-Officer—R. Richardson.

County Police—James Kidd, superintendent.

Station Agent—W. Winton. Gas Manager—William Peattie.

Agricultural Society—John Stewart, solicitor.

Dunblane Institute—P. M'Gregor, hon. secretary and treasurer;
J. Robertson, librarian.

School Management Committee—A. H. Anderson, chairman;
A. B. Barty, clerk.

Solicitors—J. A. M'Lean, James Barty, LL.B., A. B. Barty,
LL.B., and John Stewart.

Freemasons' Lodge (The Lodge of Dunblane, No. IX.)—James
Sharp, R.W.M.; A. J. Low, secretary; J. C. Waddell,
treasurer.

Provincial Grand Lodge of Perthshire West—Colonel A. M. B.
Grahame of Glenny, P.G.M.; Alexander Liles, Main street,
Callander, secy.

Parish Council—Col. A. W. Hay Drummond, chairman; Inspector, Clerk and Registrar, John C. Waddell.

Police Commissioners—D. C. Blair, provost; Robt. Thomas
and Charles Angus, bailies; D. T. Reid, clerk; J. A.
M'Lean, burgh chamberlain; John Stewart, solicitor,
burgh prosecutor; Alexander M'Gillivray, collector; John
Porter, burgh surveyor.

DUNKELD.

Resident Justices of the Peace—Wm. Cox of Snaigow; J. Speed,
Forneth; W. S. Fothringham of Murthly; Lord Dunedin
of Stenton; David Watson, baron bailie, ex officio; A. E.
Cox, of Dungarthill; James Paton, Obney, Bankfoot;
R. M'Gillewie, Dunkeld.

Clergy—Rev. Thomas R. Rutherford, Established; Rev. John
W. Hamilton, United Free.

Teachers—Henry Crombie, M.A., rector of Royal Grammar
School, Misses Stewart, M'Ilwrick, Edward, Hean, Low,
and Warren, assistants.

Collector of Bishop's Rents—Office of Woods, &c.

Bankers—Bank of Scotland, T. A. Peacock, agent; Union Bank
of Scotland, R. M'Gillewie, agent; Savings Bank, Archibald Buchanan, agent.

Medical Men—Dr. Mathers, J. Anderson Taylor, M.D.

Post and Telegraph Office—Angus Macpherson, postmaster.

Stamps and Taxes—

Session-Clerk and treasurer—The Rev. T. R. Rutherford.

Inspector of Poor and Collector, and Registrar — George Stewart.

Parish Council—Alex. Campbell, Tullymully, chairman; J. Roberts, John Brodie, Jas. Conacher, C. Scott (Dowally), Andrew Jack, Edward Miller, P. Kennedy. and Andrew Smith.

Reading Room—Pres., J. M'Rostie ; secy. and treas., John F. Stewart.

Dunkeld Curling Club (Dunkeld Division)—Duke of Atholl, K.T., M.V.O., D.S.O., president; R. M'Gillewie, Dunkeld, vice-president; Alex. Campbell, secretary and treasurer.

Inns and Hotels—Duke of Atholl Arms, Public Houses Trust Coy., Royal Hotel, Mrs. Malcolm ; Perth Arms, D. M. Dow ; Atholl Tavern, Miss Henry.

Gas Work—Secretary, John Jackson ; manager, W. R. Lawson.

Highland Railway—Opened September, 1863; trains run between Dunkeld and Perth several times daily, and to Inverness twice a day ; A. Fraser, agent.

City Hall Trust—A. Buchanan, secretary.

County Police—Duncan Campbell.

County Councillor—Robert Inglis

Masonic Lodges—(Lodge of Dunkeld, St. John's, No. 14)— Rev. C. M. Robertson, R.W.M.; Daniel Bethune, secretary and treasurer. (Lodge Operative, No. 152)—Joseph Sim, R.W.M.; William Jack, secy.; William Jack, treas. •

Dunkeld and Birnam Mercantile Association—Pres., Wm Bain, vice-pres., R. Scott; secy., Geo. Stewart ; treas., D. Macpherson.

DUNNING.

Resident Justices of the Peace—Lord Rollo and Dunning, and Dr. Donaldson.

Ministers—Rev. Peter Thomson, D.D., and Rev. Edwin M. M. Davidson, Parish Church ; Rev. J. M. Jeffray, United Free Church ; Rev. Thomas Watt, Townhead Manse.

Session-Clerk—Robt. Mathews,   Registrar—Wm. Brown.

Medical—Dr. G. Donaldson, Dr. Brown Watt.

Postmistress—Miss Drewitt.

County Council Representative—Lord Rollo.

County Police Constable—William Hutchison.

Teachers—W. Kerr, M.A., Public School ; Miss Philp, Infants.

Inspector of Poor—Wm. Brown.

Heritors Clerk—William Henderson.

Mutual Improvement Society and Recreation Society—President, Rev. E. M. M. Davidson ; secretary, Charles Laing ; treasurer, Miss Sword.

Parish Council—Lord Rollo, Chairman; R. Mathews, vice-chairman. Wm. Brown, clerk.

Reading-Room and Library—Wm. Kerr, M.A., librarian; Mrs. Laing, caretaker.

Carrier—

Bankers—Wm. Brown, for Union Bank of Scotland (Limited).

Weekly Market—Wednesday.

Savings Bank—Wm. Brown, cashier.

Curling Club—Hon. Lord Rollo, president; Angus Howie secretary; J. Dougall, treasurer.

ERROL.

Superior of Village—Lady Ogilvy Dalgleish of Errol.

Resident Justices of Peace — Lord Kinnaird of Rossie; Captain Malcolm Drummond of Megginch; Colonel Drummond Hay of Seggieden; Guy E. Broun-Morison, of Murie; C. J. G. F. Paterson of Castle Huntly; Alex. Prain, 79 Colinton Road, Edinburgh; John Prain, Inver-gowrie; Jas. Kidd, Mains Errol; George Bell, South Inch-michael, Errol; Wm. Niven, Loan, Errol.

Ministers—Established, Rev. Kenneth D. M'Laren; United Free—Vacant.

Teachers—Robert Strathdee, Public; Mrs. C. B. Taylor, Glen-doick, Public.

Medical Men—John Liddell.

Banker—W. Goodall, agent for Union Bank of Scotland, Ltd.

Postmaster—A. Burden; sub-office, Miss N.Symon, postmistress.

Session-Clerk—James Bruce.

Registrar—David Nicoll.

Parish Council—D. Nicoll, inspector; Wm .Goodall, collector.

Reading-Room and Library—David Nicoll, librarian; Wm. Goodall, secretary and treasurer.

Markets—Last Wed. of July, and Wed. before Little Dunning.

KILLIN.

Resident Justices of the Peace—P. Stewart, draper; J. D. M'Rae, auctioneer; John M'Diarmid, Draper.

Clergy—George W. Mackay, Established; Duncan MacGregor U.F.

Killin Institute (Reading & Recreation Rooms)—J. D. M'Rae, convener; Peter Ross, secretary; Sergt. P. M'Rae, keeper.

Killin Curling Club—Marquis of Breadalbane, K.G., patron; P. Stewart, president; Donald M'Laren, secretary.

Killin Angling Club—Douglas Willison, president; John Macdiarmid, hon. secretary and treasurer.

Killin Football Club—Marquis of Breadalbane. K.G., patron; Marquis of Tullibardine, M.P., hon. president; W. Wilson, secretary.

Killin Bowling Club—Marquis of Breadalbane, K.G., patron; Peter Ross, secretary.

Public School—James M'Raw, M.A., headmaster; assistant, Miss Craig; Miss Reid, infant mistress.

Banks—Bank of Scotland, E. MacEwen, agent; J. Guthrie, accountant; Union Bank of Scotland, Limited, Peter M'Neil, agent; John Campbell, accountant.

Postmaster—Henry Horwood. Letters despatched twice daily to all parts, and received once daily from all parts.

Sub-Distr. of Stamps & Sub-Collector of Taxes—H. Horwood.

Medical—Dr. A. D. Wilson.

School Board—J. D. M'Rae, member Education Authority, chairman; P. Stewart, clerk.

Parish Council—John M'Diarmid, chairman; Peter Stewart, inspector, collector, and clerk.

Registrar—Wm. Walker.

Markets—January, first Tuesday after 11th; May, on 5th, excepting it fall on Saturday, Sunday, or Monday, when it is kept on the Tues. following; Nov., first Tues. after 11th.

Cattle and Sheep Sales—Fortnightly. M'William & M'Rae, auctioneers.

Killin Railway Company—The Most Hon. the Marquis of Breadalbane, chairman; Ewen MacEwen, secretary.

Sanitary Inspector—Mr. Low, Dunblane.

Estate Agent—Ewen MacEwen, factor for Capt. W. L. Christie of Loch Dochart, and for Captain Place of Crianlarich.

METHVEN.

Resident Justices of the Peace—Col. Smythe of Methven, Dr. Alexander Johnston, Methven; Thos. Young, Newbigging; John Graham, Tippermallo; T. W. Reid, Methven.

Parish Council—Methven Ward—T. W. Reid, J. F. Donaldsen, Andrew Smith, Alex. Johnston, J. Graham, J. Keay, T. Young. Almondbank Ward—Col. Smythe and J. Paterson.

Clergy—Rev. James Robertson, D.S.O., D.D., Established; Rev. George Williams, United Free; Rev. J. Keenan (Crieff), Catholic.

Teachers—Public School, Duncan M. Carmichael, M.A., headmaster; Miss O. Blyth, infant mistress.

Medical—Dr. Alex. Johnston, Methven, and Dr. O. Johnston, Methven.

Session-Clerk—T. W. Reid. Postmaster—Thomas W. Reid

Registrar—Thos. E. Robertson. County Police—P. C. Blyth

Inspector of Poor and Collector, Sub. Sanitary Inspector for Tibbermore, Methven, Gask, Aberdalgie, and Perth (Landward)—Thomas E. Robertson.

Curling Club—Col. Smythe of Methven, patron; Mrs. Smythe of Methven, patroness; Col. Smythe of Methven, president; Geo. Pople, vice-president; Mr. Pople, Newhouse, representative member; Mr. John Graham, secretary.

Bowling Club—Mrs. Smythe of Methven, patroness; Col. Smythe of Methven, patron; John Graham, president; Dr. Johnston, Methven, vice-president; Thomas Robertson, sec.; A. Scrimgeour, treas.

Subscription Library—Duncan M. Carmichael, M.A., librarian.

School Committee of Management—Rev. R. G. Macdonald, chairman; Rev. J. E. M'Ouat, J. E. Adamson, J. Paterson, J. Stalker, J. F. Donaldson, G. L. Brown, R. Jack, D. Campbell.

County Council Representative—Col. Smythe.

MUTHILL.

Resident Justices of the Peace—Robert T. N. Speir of Culdees, G. T. Ewing, Pitkellony, and John C. D. Irvine, M.B., Kirklea.

Clergy—Rev. A. Cross, M.A., Established; Rev. R. P. R. Anderson, M.A., U.F.; Rev. A. B. Caird, Episcopal.

Public Teachers—John Gow, F.E.I.S., Miss Lily Clark, Miss A. Diack, Miss E. Ingram; Mrs. Campbell, Blairinroar.

Postmistress—Elizabeth Byth. County Police—Jas. M'Pherson

Heritors' Clerk—Malcolm Finlayson, solicitor, Crieff.

Session-Clerk—John Gow.

Parochial Medical Officer—John C. D. Irvine, M.B.

Earl of Ancaster's Library—Robert Inkster, librarian.

Parish Council—George T. Ewing, chairman; P. G. M'Ara, inspector of poor, and collector.

Registrar—Andrew Black.

Muthill Curling Club—R. Muir, secy.; P. M'Neill, treas.

Drummond Castle Curling Club—Alexander Brydie, secretary and treasurer.

Masons' Lodge, St. John's—Robert Inkster, R.W.M.

District Nurse—Miss Adams.

Muthill Bowling Club—Lachlan Tainsh, secretary.

Golf Club—Geo. Stuart, secretary.

Boy Scouts—Rev. R. P. R. Anderson, scoutmaster.

Recreation Club—Rev. A. Cross, M.A., Secretary.

PITLOCHRY.

Resident Justices of the Peace—Alex. B. Stewart of Balnakeilly; Hugh Mitchell, Pitlochry; D. Stewart Fergusson of Dunfallandy; Henry Smith, Pitlochry; C. A. Miller, Craigholm, W. Fenton, Pitlochry; Alexander MacBeth, Pitlochry, and A. M. Meldrum, solicitor.

Bankers—Bank of Scotland, R. T. M. Sinclair, agent; Commercial Bank of Scotland, D. R. Mackay, agent; Union Bank of Scotland, H. Mitchell, B. W. Liddell, and A. M. Meldrum, agents; Perth Savings Bank—H. Mitchell, cashier.

Inland Revenue—Mr. George P. Warren, supervisor.

Clergy—Rev. D. M'Alister Donald, Established Church ; Rev. Arch. J. Macnicol, U.F. ; Episcopal, Rev. H. M'Naught; Baptist, Rev. W. M'Lauchlan.

Medical—S. Beatty, M.B.C M., John Anderson, M.B.C.M. and C. H. Newton, M.B.Ch.B.

Postmaster, Stamps, and Taxes — J. Scott.

Registrar—James Finlay, Moulin. Strathloch District—Peter Michie, Glenshee. Tenandry District—Thos. M'Glashan, M.A., J.P.

Teachers—W. MacGowan, M.A., and Miss Butter.

Solicitors and Notaries Public—J. & H. Mitchell, A. Macbeth, B. W. Liddell, W.S., A. M. Meldrum, and C. H. Gordon.

Highland District Council—Hugh Mitchell and B. W. Liddell, joint clerks, treasurers and collectors.

Auctioneers and Licensed Appraiser—Robert Robertson.

Markets—Cattle and horses, Saturday before first Wednesday, May ; sheep, third Tuesday of August ; cattle and horses, third Wednesday (o.s.) October.

Stationmaster—Daniel Fraser.

Public Hall, Pitlochry—W. Panton, Union Bank, secy.

Parish Council—Hugh Mitchell, clerk ; R. H. Stewart, inspector.

Pitlochry School Management Committee—A. M. Meldrum, clerk.

Pitlochry Gas Company—Hugh Mitchell, secretary.

RATTRAY.

Provost of Rattray—Wm. Scott ; clerk, James M. Hodge, solicitor ; Depute Clerk, Wm. Turnbull ; treasurer, W. S. Neish.

Resident Justices of Peace—George Bisset, Colonel P. Burn Clerk Rattray, J. M. Hodge.

Clergy — Established, Rev. W. D. Fyfe, M.A., B.D. ; U.F., Rev. A. Macrae ; Wesleyan, Rev. Mr. Leedal.

Teachers—C. H. Owen, M.A., headmaster ; T. Fyffe, Chas. Sim, Miss Mitchell, Miss Harris, Miss Michie ; Miss Doig, Miss Farquharson, Miss Banks.

Session-Clerk—W. S. Neish.   Registrar—W. S. Neish.

Parish Council — Wm. Proctor, chairman ; John Stewart, solicitor, clerk.   Inspector of Poor—W. S. Neish.

Post Office—Miss Grant, New Rattray ; and Mrs. Mitchell, Westfields.

PRINTED BY JAMES H. JACKSON, 26 HIGH STREET, PERTH.

Index

Printed in the United Kingdom
by Lightning Source UK Ltd.
103319UKS00002B/98